ENGLISH BLUE AND WHITE PORCELAIN OF THE 18th CENTURY

KU-367-380

WORCESTER BEAKER. Height, 8 in. Open crescent mark. About 1760.

A choice specimen of the painted ware decorated with slender "Long Elizas". The beauty of the foliate scrolls should be noted, together with the typical Worcester borders at the rim and base.

ENGLISH BLUE AND WHITE PORCELAIN OF THE 18TH CENTURY

*An illustrated descriptive account of the early soft paste
productions of Bow, Chelsea, Lowestoft, Derby,
Longton Hall, Bristol, Worcester, Caughley,
and Liverpool Potters, circa 1740–1800*

By
STANLEY W. FISHER

WITH A FOREWORD BY
BERNARD RACKHAM

LONDON
B. T. BATSFORD LTD.
15 North Audley Street, W.1

STIRLING
DISTRICT
LIBRARY

First published 1947

738.2
/FIS

195165

MADE AND PRINTED IN GREAT BRITAIN UNDER THE DIRECTION
OF THE PUBLISHERS, B. T. BATSFORD, LIMITED, LONDON, W.I, BY
WILLIAM CLOWES AND SONS, LIMITED, LONDON AND BECCLES

DEDICATED

BY GRACIOUS PERMISSION

TO

HER MAJESTY QUEEN MARY

FOREWORD
BY
BERNARD RACKHAM

CHINESE PORCELAIN BECAME familiar in England as in other parts of Europe first in the form of "blue and white", porcelain, that is, with decoration painted in cobalt on the "biscuit"—the unfired "body"— before the application of the glaze and fired at the same time with it. Well acquainted as we are with blue patterns as one of the commonest forms of decoration on our ordinary domestic pottery of to-day, it is not easy to realise that, in our country, as late as the time of Shakespeare, such a thing was quite unknown to any but a favoured few; those who, like Lord Burleigh, came into possession of pieces of the almost fabulous translucent wares then beginning to make their way into England from the East, regarded them as so precious that they mounted in costly settings of silver gilt articles which by the Chinese themselves would have been little regarded, as routine products of their kilns, made expressly to be exported abroad. In England, as elsewhere in Europe, the attractions of these Chinese wares so quickly won favour that home potters were compelled in self-defence to discover how best they could compete with them. What we know as "English delft"—the tin-glazed earthenware made chiefly in London and Bristol—for more than a century represented the best that could be done in the way of imitation. When at last porcelain itself, a translucent ware simulating the outward appearance of the Chinese but entirely different from it in composition, began to be made in small factories started by private enterprise, Germany and France had already entered the field several decades earlier; thanks largely to princely patronage, they had thriving manufactures not only of blue and white, but also of the more splendid enamel-painted porcelains, inspired partly by the polychrome wares which were by that time added to the output of Japanese as well as Chinese exporters, but also partly by the Western art of the enameller on glass and metal.

FOREWORD

Anyone paying even a cursory visit to a museum in which the Continental as well as the English porcelains are adequately represented cannot fail, if at all observant, to be struck by the fact that, whilst in the cabinets devoted to the latter class blue and white is to be found only here and there, in those of the former it constitutes quite a large proportion of the exhibits. On closer inspection he is likely to feel that, with the possible exception of the blue and white of St. Cloud and Rouen and the still earlier precocious products of Florentine experiment, the Continental examples are somewhat unsympathetic and devoid of attractiveness; this is because they are of true, "hard paste" porcelain, and their makers never mastered the skill in preparation and firing of the pigment which in China bore fruit in such lovely and varied hues. Among the products of the English factories, on the other hand, owing to the very fact that they are the result of a diversity of technical practice, he will find a variety almost equal to that of the Oriental, if never quite rivalling its surpassing beauty. Blue and white may, therefore, be regarded as one of the specialities of English porcelain manufacture in the eighteenth century. Chelsea was the only factory which almost entirely neglected it, and Chelsea, it may be pointed out, was established by foreigners and aimed almost exclusively at competition with the most splendid of its Continental rivals. Also, towards the end of the century, blue and white began to lose favour with the world of fashion, so that its production was left to the minor factories such as Lowestoft and Caughley, and Worcester, which at the outset had given to it so much attention and excelled in its production, abandoned it in favour of something more showy.

It is perhaps a symptom of the more sober taste prevalent in England as compared with the Continent that blue and white was so much in favour. It harmonises to perfection with the comfortable mahogany of Chippendale and Sheraton and with the quiet dignity of English silver plate. Its appreciation may well be a measure of the good judgment of the growing body of collectors who will find such admirable guidance in the following pages.

B. R.

Guildford, 1947.

AUTHOR'S PREFACE

BLUE AND WHITE porcelain quite erroneously and incomprehensibly has been pushed back too far in all works on porcelain, and it is high time that it was brought to the front for an honest and deserved appreciation. That it has charm and beauty is undeniable; it "marries" with any decorative scheme, old or new; and its progress visualises the unfolding of home-history itself. It is utilitarian. It exhales humanity. It is unobtrusive—it speaks quietly though insistently, but does not shout. Nevertheless, man searches out instinctively the rarer or less common objects, and maybe often chooses snobbishly. But at heart the love remains for the shyer sister, the gentle maiden "sprig-muslin drest", even while he is captivated by a more sophisticated charmer.

It might certainly be supposed that absence of colour other than blue must limit the æsthetic appeal which is the greatest charm of a piece of porcelain. This is not so, however, since the very absence of varied colour necessitates a more rigid control of design; and the artist, realising his limited means of expression, must perforce exercise greater care in making his designs effective and subtle in conception, since it is in this way only that he is able to give beauty to his creation. The fact that, as we shall see, the English artist was to a large extent a mere copyist or at best a translator of foreign ideas has little bearing on the point, since the originators had in most cases already successfully overcome their limitations.

Inevitably such a book as this must be largely a compilation of known facts rather than the revelation of new, but I hope that even connoisseurs may gain some new knowledge from my pages, though I write, primarily, for the beginner. It is for him that I have chosen the diagrams and the photographs with which the text is illustrated. I have included no museum pieces and none which by reason of extreme rarity or value would be out of reach of the collector of moderate

2

means. Nowadays collecting is becoming the hobby of a larger circle than in the past, and it is my hope that these pages may be the humble means of introducing many more lovers of the beautiful in art to the joys of collecting Old English porcelain.

I should like to place on record that in no small measure the writing of this book is a tribute to the knowledge and fine enthusiasm of my old friend Conrad H. Tipping, B.A., F.R.Hist.S., whose ever-ready help and constructive criticism have been an inspiration at all times. My grateful thanks are also due to Mr. Bernard Rackham for so kindly contributing the Foreword, and to my Publishers, especially their Director, Mr. W. Hanneford-Smith, F.R.S.(Edin.), for their guidance and enthusiastic collaboration.

S. W. F.

Bewdley,
   Worcestershire.

CONTENTS

CHAP.   PAGE

       FOREWORD by Bernard Rackham   vii

       AUTHOR'S PREFACE   ix

       LIST OF PLATES   xiii

   I   INTRODUCTION   I

  II   DECORATION   7

 III   BOW   23

  IV   CHELSEA   35

   V   LOWESTOFT   42

  VI   DERBY   49

 VII   LONGTON HALL   60

VIII   BRISTOL (REDCLIFF BACKS)   68

  IX   WORCESTER   76

   X   CAUGHLEY   119

  XI   LIVERPOOL   140

 XII   ON COLLECTING   155

XIII   MARKS   160

XIV   NOTES ON MATERIALS, MANUFACTURE, AND
          DECORATION   169

       CHRONOLOGY   182, 183

       BIBLIOGRAPHY   184

       INDEX   185

EXPLANATORY NOTE RESPECTING THE PLATES INCLUDED IN THIS VOLUME

No matter how much care may be taken either in the selection or in the treatment of specimens chosen to illustrate a book of this description, the value of any photograph is clearly limited, inasmuch as reproduction is restricted to shape and decoration. If it were practicable to photograph all the specimens in true colour the value of the illustrations would be greatly increased, because the tone of blue used in the decoration is of immense value in diagnosis. Rather than represent all the pieces in colour which might not be absolutely accurate and so defeat my object, therefore, I have chosen to include four colour plates only, and I believe that they are faithful reproductions. I have deemed it advisable to supplement the plates with detailed explanations, which I trust will help the reader to gain a better understanding of the specimens reproduced. All of them are of the type well within the reach of the average collector—indeed, with two exceptions, they are all from my own collection.

LIST OF PLATES

PLATE   PAGE

1 Worcester Beaker, painted with foliate scrolls together with typical borders at the rim and base (*In colour*)   *Frontispiece*

VARIOUS FACTORIES

2 Small round dishes (Liverpool and Worcester), decorated in various styles; and powder-blue plates with reserves (Worcester, Caughley, and Bow). All painted   11

3 Cylindrical mugs (Worcester, Caughley, and Liverpool), showing styles of early decoration in both painting and printing   12

4 Pickle or sweet-meat trays in leaf and shell form (Lowestoft, Worcester, Longton Hall, and Caughley). Painted and printed   17

5 Globular tea-pots (Worcester, Lowestoft, and Caughley), decorated with painted landscapes in Chinese style and printed "Fisherman" pattern   18

BOW

6 Bow dish, painted in Chinese style with "Image" pattern (*In colour*)   22

7 Table-wares, painted in Chinese style, showing various classes of decoration   26

8 Sauce-boat, painted in pale blue in Chinese style. Peony decoration   31

9 Mug, bell-shape, peony decoration, heart-shaped handle terminal   32

CHELSEA

10 Hexagonal bowl, painted in Chinese style   37

LOWESTOFT

11 Coffee-pot, painted in powder blue, with reserves (*In colour*)   43

12 Table-wares, typical mouldings and styles of decoration. Painted and printed   44

DERBY

13 Openwork basket, painted in Chinese style, with applied flowers; and coffee-cup painted with "Long Elizas"   51

14 Plate, painted in Chinese style with dragons and bats   52

LIST OF PLATES

PLATE   PAGE

CHELSEA-DERBY

15   Sauce-boat, moulded, and painted in Chinese style with brocade and diaper ornament, flowers, and landscape. Blue cross mark   57

LONGTON HALL

16   Mug, moulded, of typical shape; and cups, showing Littler's "streaky" blue, and two sorts of glaze   63

17   Tea-bowl and saucer, painted "exotic birds", printed Liverpool border   64

REDCLIFF BACKS

18   Hexagonal Butter-boat, painted Chinese figures and emblems; and bowl, decorated flowers   73

WORCESTER

19   Cornucopia, moulded and painted with flowers in the Meissen style (*In colour*)   77

20   Cornucopia, moulded, and painted with flowers and diaper   81

21   Dish, painted "Hundred Antiques"   82

22   Egg-drainer, spoon-shaped, painted decoration in Chinese style; and coffee-cup, Chinese figures, moulded scroll handle   87

23   Bell-shaped mugs, Chinese "root decoration"; and two-handled sauce-boat, Chinese landscape and flowers   88

24   Cream-jug and sauce-boats, moulded in various styles, painted in Chinese style   93

25   Coffee-cup, mug, and cream-jug, painted with "Long Elizas"; and coffee-pots, painted and printed in various styles   94

26   Tea-bowls, coffee-cups and saucers, various styles of moulded and painted decoration   97

27   Bowl, painted with Chinese landscape; and jug, "cabbage-leaf" moulding, painted in Meissen style   98

28   Mug, cylindrical, painted "cracked ice and prunus" pattern, with "Long Elizas" in reserves   103

29   Bowl, unusual Chinese decoration; and sucrier, painted with flowers   104

30   Cress-dish, pierced, and painted flowers; and plate, wickerwork moulding with "Chantilly sprig" decoration   107

31   Spittoon, with printed flowers; and jug, "cabbage-leaf" moulding with mask lip, printed fruit and flowers   108

32   Tea-bowl and saucer, printed "Two Milkmaids" pattern in blue   111

33   Plates, printed styles; and feeding-cup, printed flowers   112

LIST OF PLATES

PLATE   PAGE

34   Salad-bowl, printed fruit, flowers, and vegetables; and coffee-cups and saucers printed in various styles   115

35   Tea-pot, moulded, painted "Royal Lily" pattern, Flight period   116

CAUGHLEY

36   Tea-bowl, coffee-cup, saucers, and cream jugs, printed in various styles   121

37   Mug, a rare "Trial piece", painted with Chinese scenes, and bearing the date 22nd May, 1787   122

38   Jug, "cabbage-leaf" moulding and mask lip, printed with "Parrot and Vine" decoration   127

39   Dessert-dish, moulded, powder-blue, with Chinese flowers, emblems, and diaper in reserves and in the bottom   128

40   Butter-dishes and covers and stands, oval and cylindrical styles, with printed decoration   131

41   Mugs, cylindrical, one with initials and date, painted; the other printed. "Chantilly sprig" decoration   137

LIVERPOOL (Zachariah Barnes)

42   Pickle-shell, pounce-pot, and mug, with printed decoration typical of the factory   143

LIVERPOOL (Barnes and Chaffers)

43   Tea-pot, decorated flowers and characteristic Barnes border; and tea-bowls, coffee-cup, and saucers printed and painted in various styles   144

LIVERPOOL (Chaffers)

44   Bowl, painted flowers, and coffee-cup, moulded   149

LIVERPOOL (Pennington)

45   Coffee-cup and saucer, octagonal, painted "Jumping boy" pattern   150

Chapter I

INTRODUCTION

IT IS necessary before any attempt is made to discuss porcelain to define as closely as possible the nature of its body. This may be either of two kinds, which may be referred to as True Porcelain and Artificial Porcelain. True Porcelain was probably discovered by the Chinese during the fourth or fifth century, although there is little direct evidence to support the assumption, and consists of a mixture of china stone (or petuntse) and china clay (or kaolin) in varying proportions. The fused result is an extremely hard material, resistant to very high temperatures and to abrasion by a steel instrument such as a knife or file. This body is usually known as Hard Paste or True Porcelain. Artificial Porcelain, or Soft Paste, was the result of endless experiments which were undertaken with a view to the successful manufacture of a similar translucent substance. Eventually some form of translucency was attained by the mixing of an actual glass (or Fritt) in a powdered state with some form of white clay. The result was a material which was not resistant to any great degree of heat, and which was easily scratched by a knife or a file.

It is the latter class of porcelain with which I intend to deal. My chief reason for this is that it forms by far the greater part of blue and white porcelain made in England during the eighteenth century. In addition, lovers of porcelain usually have a decided preference for either hard or soft paste, so that a collector of Chinese porcelain usually finds difficulty in understanding the soft paste imitation. It should be appreciated also that soft paste fritt porcelain is fundamentally English; its very failings often helping to make an irresistible appeal to the senses. There is something very restful about it which is lacking in its more glittering, polished, one might almost say ultra-perfect, relation.

Soft paste porcelain was evolved on the Continent at Florence during the sixteenth century, and about the end of the seventeenth

3   I

century was produced in large quantities in France, whence the art spread to this country in the mid-eighteenth century. Naturally enough, at a period when experiment was the rule and there was little real knowledge, there was a great variety of formulæ, and it is difficult to state with any degree of accuracy what mixtures were used at any specific factory. As will be seen later, however, certain preferences were evolved. Thus, whereas the earliest English porcelains are said to have been made of glass, sand, and pipe-clay, it was not long before soapstone or steatite was used at Bristol, Worcester, Liverpool, and Caughley, and bone ash at Chelsea, Bow, Derby, and Lowestoft, with resultant improvements in fire-resisting qualities. At a later date the latter constituent was an important ingredient in a new paste discovered by Josiah Spode towards the end of the eighteenth century. He abandoned the use of a fritt and made a body of china stone, china clay, and a large proportion of bone ash. This quickly proved its worth as far as ease of manufacture and serviceability were concerned, and it was soon adopted throughout the industry. With the standardisation of paste our study will end at the close of the eighteenth century, after which, apart from questions of decoration, interest inevitably wanes.

Little need be said at this stage concerning the glaze which is found on the surface of all soft porcelains. A glaze is simply a very thin covering of some form of glass, containing either lead or oxide of tin, added to the baked porcelain (then known as biscuit) in a state of suspension in powdered form in water, and fired in an oven at a comparatively low temperature.

By "blue and white" I mean porcelain which is decorated on the biscuit beneath the glaze and, therefore, termed "underglaze blue". The blue invariably used was cobalt blue. No other colour, with the exception of manganese purple and copper red, was able to withstand the high kiln-temperature, and, in addition, the ware which the English potters first attempted to imitate was the Chinese blue and white imported into England in vast quantities at that time, and painted in a similar cobalt blue. The use of cobalt as a decorative medium was understood by the Chinese as early as the seventh century, when the ore was finely divided, painted on the body in the desired design, and covered by a colourless glaze. Porcelain decorated in this way reached perfection during the reign of the Emperor K'hang H'si (1662–1723), by which time the methods of purification of the ore had been perfected. At its best, the blue and white of this period has the beautiful ivory tone of curdled milk, which is enhanced by the sapphire tone of the blue. Strangely enough, however, in England at any rate, it appears that absolute purity of the ore was not essential to the best results, since some of the old-established potteries fail to-day to reproduce as good cobalt as they did in the olden days, using the old recipes, worked under modern and better methods. The results are harsher, and lacking in the old distinctive warm tone—due, surely, to over-purification of the ore. Whether decorated by means of printing or painting, and using pigments of varying purity, all of which were made from cobalt ore, blue and white porcelain was produced in extremely large quantities by the porcelain factories at Bow, Chelsea, Derby, Bristol (Redcliff Backs Factory), Worcester, Caughley, Liverpool, Lowestoft, and Longton Hall.

Apart from a necessary reference to the history of the factories and to the potters themselves, it is natural and necessary that the identification of the various porcelains should form an important part of any study of porcelain. Correct diagnosis is a satisfaction which enhances the joy of possession, although it should not be looked upon as the be-all and end-all of collecting. The factors governing identification are paste (the body of which the porcelain is made), glaze, form, and decoration. Although these features will be dealt with in detail in later chapters it will be as well to make general reference to them here. We have seen that there were many recipes, and it follows that, in conjunction with the glaze, the various porcelains will have their own individual variations. Care must be taken, nevertheless, to avoid stressing them unduly, since experiment was continually going on, and there was little or no standardisation. Early Worcester paste was usually creamy white, but with a greenish hue when held against artificial light, caused by the admixture of cobalt blue to the glaze which was intended to give a bluish cast in imitation of the Chinese ware which was copied. Since the glaze was brushed on, exposed patches of uncovered biscuit paste inside the foot rim are usual, but are not a reliable indication of Worcester origin, since the same procedure was

3

adopted by other factories. Caughley porcelain, on the other hand, is cloudy orange or straw-coloured by transmitted light. Chelsea paste has round or semi-circular patches of extra translucency caused by unmixed quantities of glassy fritt, intentional or otherwise, and so on; characteristics to remember, but not to labour, since, as we shall see, they were shared by other factories.

In addition to paste and glaze we find characteristics of manufacture, among which is the shape of the foot rim. Thus the inside of many Liverpool foot rims is undercut, whereas Worcester foot rims are triangular and Caughley rectangular in section, and there may be no foot rim at all to many pieces of Bow and Derby. Specially shaped handles were used, as in the case of the "biting snake" of Liverpool and Worcester, and the heart-shaped lower terminal on many specimens of Bow, both of which will be fully considered later, together with many others. It was the custom to make extensive use of silver shapes in the manufacture of moulded pieces such as sauce-boats, cream-jugs, coffee-pots, and jugs; but as it was a simple matter to make a plaster mould of any article, it is common to find pieces of different origin cast in what is apparently the same mould, alike in every minute detail. With few exceptions, therefore, which will be noted, it is dangerous to rely on moulding as conclusive evidence of origin.

Last, but by no means least, is identification by means of decoration. Here is treacherous ground indeed! The decorator of those early days was a nomadic creature, making his way from place to place taking with him not only his own individual style, but also ideas and designs which he had learnt during his wanderings. Again, although much originality was often displayed in early decoration, it was nevertheless the custom to copy from the Chinese, and similar or even identical patterns are to be found on specimens of different manufacture. Thus again, with certain reservations, identification by decoration alone is impossible.

What of marks? What has been said of decoration is true also of marks. Although certain factories adopted signs or symbols as trade marks, these were often copies of marks upon Chinese or Continental models, since the article was copied in its entirety, marks as well. In such cases it is an open question whether deceit was intended. It may be that factories really wished to sell their own productions as genuine Chinese or Meissen (Dresden), or even as the work of a rival factory. On the other hand, it must be remembered that factories of repute were frequently called upon to replace parts of a damaged service, in which case it would be natural to copy the original mark.

To sum up, the only sure method of identification is by means of a careful examination of all the factors we have considered, paste, glaze, form, and decoration. Is the specimen, in the first place, soft paste? If so, it will become warm to the tongue or cheek very quickly, and it will be soft to the touch, especially on the base of the foot rim, which will not scratch the finger-nail, but which, on the other hand, will be easily marked with a knife point or a file (provided you are reckless or unsympathetic enough to attempt such sacrilege!). Should the edge be chipped the fracture will be rough and granulated to the touch, but it will not mark the nail. There will be no tiny pits or pin poison in the glaze, which is often badly scratched with continual use, allowing the paste to become stained by the liquids which the article has contained. Occasionally a harder glaze was used, however, in order to support a particularly fragile paste, so that it is unwise to rely solely on the evidence of scratches. Often you may be able to see through the glaze as through a piece of glass, especially if the surface of the specimen is covered with a film of dust, in which case the thickness of the glaze may sometimes be seen. The glaze on hard paste, on the contrary, was fired with the paste and hence became part of it. Soft paste is porous, so that colours tend to sink into the body, or to run in the glaze; the edges of the brush strokes are rarely well defined. If the piece is held aslant to the light, the glaze will be as shiny over the coloured parts as over the uncoloured; if it were hard paste the glaze over the decoration would be rather dull.

Examine the paste and glaze, both in daylight and against a strong artificial light, preferably through a small hole in a sheet of cardboard. Note its colour and quality, and whether the glaze is thickly or thinly applied; whether clean, or disfigured by black specks or sand; whether close fitting, or inclined to run into pools or lumps. Form, moulding, and special modelling characteristics should then be examined, together with the style of decoration, and whether painted or printed. By this time one should have a good idea of the origin and date of the piece, and then, and only then, the mark may be examined as a final deciding factor to clinch the matter. This procedure, lengthy though it may appear to be, is the only practical method of identification. As knowledge and experience are gained one is able to identify a specimen without conscious thought, and almost without appreciating the reasons which led to such identification.

Reference must be made here to methods of identification by means of chemical analysis, by means of which it is possible to separate porcelain into several classes; since bone ash and soapstone, for example, will give different chemical reactions. I do not propose, however, to make more than passing mention of these methods. To me it is in some way repugnant to make a science of what should surely be an artistic pursuit. For those who wish to inquire further, therefore, I have given particulars in another part of this book of where the necessary information can be found.*

* See p. 174, note 10.

Chapter II

DECORATION

BLUE AND WHITE porcelain may be either painted or printed. The invention of printing on porcelain by means of a paper transfer which has in turn received its colour from an engraved copper plate * has been claimed by many potteries, and the evidence has been presented in detail by William Turner in his book *Transfer Printing on Enamels, Porcelain, and Pottery,* published in 1907. Let it suffice to say that it would appear that the honour for its discovery lies between the Worcester factory and the firm of Sadler and Green of Liverpool. The latter, we must conclude, was first in the field with printing on earthenware in overglaze enamels in July 1756, closely followed by Worcester in the same year. Blue underglaze printing, however, with which we are concerned, was probably introduced at Worcester later in the same year, since there is evidence to show that Richard Holdship, who left Worcester for Derby in 1759, attempted to print "blew" at the latter factory in 1764. The main interest in the introduction of underglaze printing lies in the fact that the whole process of decoration of cheap domestic ware was revolutionised by the new method; but that does not alter the fact that specimens so printed, even though they may be less valuable than painted ware, are extremely attractive and worthwhile from the collector's point of view. In thus stressing this fact I hope I shall not be misunderstood. The painted blue and white made before 1760 is artistically, sentimentally, and æsthetically superior to the transfer, but the latter has a charm of its own despite the mechanical origin of its decoration. Practically all the styles of printed decoration were imitated on the printed ware, although the earliest specimens of the latter bear underglaze decoration in blue printed from the plates which were formerly used for overglaze printing in black, lilac, or red. An example of this is the Worcester pattern known as the "Two Milk-

* See p. 169, note 1.

7

maids", executed by Robert Hancock * in both overglaze enamels and underglaze blue (the latter sometimes further embellished with touches of red), both at Worcester and at Caughley (Plate 32). It is natural that since Worcester was the birthplace of underglaze blue printing on porcelain, the greater proportion of pieces so decorated originated there and at the neighbouring factory at Caughley, although a great deal was also produced at Liverpool, for equally obvious reasons.

I have already said that Oriental porcelain served as the first models for the early English porcelain painters, as witness the names "Worcester Tonquin Manufactory" and "New Canton" as applied to the Worcester and Bow factories, and it is now time to enlarge upon this, and to set down in detail the sources from which the painters drew their inspiration. They were as follows :—

1. K'hang H'si porcelain (period 1662–1723), decorated with ceremonial and legendary subjects, landscapes and scenes from nature, fruit and flowers, scenes from literature, and domestic incidents. Among them we find many well-known patterns which have been given arbitrary names by English collectors. Thus there is a picture of Chinese warriors and jugglers known as "The Eloping Bride" (or "Love Chase"), the Warrior and Dragon often conveniently and patriotically referred to as "St. George and the Dragon"; the "Hundred Antiques", a collection of symbolic ornaments which include a jewel, a coin, books, a painting, jade, a horn cup, and an artemisia leaf (Plate 21); the "Image" pattern depicting a man holding an axe and a boy with a bundle of sticks, a popular Bow design (Plate 6); and the "Jumping Boy", also used at Bow and sometimes at Liverpool, in which a boy appears to be jumping before a seated woman (Plate 45). The dragon was a favourite subject, together with clouds and lightning, the pattern covering both outside and inside of the article in the case of bowls, cups and saucers, and trays (Plates 14 and 25). The graceful Chinese lady, usually occupied in a Chinese garden, or playing with children, was translated into a somewhat vacant elongated female, styled by the Dutch (who copied her upon their delft) "lange liszen" (slender damsels), and so by the English "Long Elizas" (Plates 13

* See p. 176, note 13.

and 25). The ever popular "Willow Pattern", more often found upon printed than upon painted wares, was merely a copy of the usual Chinese landscape, complete with temples, islands, bridges, fences, rocks, and flying birds, all drawn in Oriental manner with a complete lack of perspective (Plate 34). A very beautiful Chinese subject, white prunus (hawthorn) blossoms on a marbled blue ground known as "cracked ice", and typifying the coming of spring, was extensively copied at the Worcester factory, where Long Elizas painted in leaf-shaped reserves added much to the beauty of shapely cylindrical mugs (Plate 28). Yet another Chinese ground colour, "powder blue", produced by blowing powdered blue pigment through a bamboo tube covered with muslin at one end, was a favourite at the same factory, and also at Lowestoft, Caughley, and Bow. Plates and tea-pots were the usual articles to carry this decoration, which has fan-shaped and round reserves filled with Chinese scenes and flowers on the blue ground (Plate 2). Many designs modelled on the Chinese style are remarkably simple, sometimes even crude. The pagoda was considered essential, and was often anglicised into a church-like structure complete with diamond-paned windows and weathercock or even equipped with a belfry (Plate 12). Indeed, in practically every case some part of the design bears trace of English influence. Slavish copying of shape without an understanding of the significance of the parts of a landscape often results in unrecognisable shapes. For example, I have a pair of mugs decorated with tent-like objects which I have recently discovered to be intended for rear views of Chinese figures (Plate 3). It is, of course, understandable that repeated and mechanical copying must inevitably lead to such results.

2. Japanese porcelain. Direct Japanese influence is uncommon, but there are exceptions, the chief, and indeed the only notable one, being the "partridge" pattern, painted in the so-called Kakiemon style, and more usually rendered in colours.

3. Pseudo-Chinese influence. In the mid-eighteenth century there was a wave of great enthusiasm in France for everything pertaining to the Chinese. This was evinced in all sections of art, and even in architecture. The movement spread to this country, as witness the erection about 1757 of the Pagoda at Kew, and the making of Chinese gardens

PLATE 2

VARIOUS FACTORIES

a DISH. LIVERPOOL (Chaffers). Diameter, 4 in. Unmarked. About 1765–70.

b DISH. WORCESTER. Diameter, 4½ in. Workman's mark. About 1765.

c DISH. WORCESTER. Diameter, 4 in. Workman's mark. About 1760–65.

d PLATE. WORCESTER. Diameter, 7½ in. Simulated Chinese mark. About 1760.

e PLATE. CAUGHLEY. Diameter, 7½ in. Simulated Chinese mark and SALOPIAN impressed. About 1775.

f PLATE. BOW. Diameter, 6¾ in. Simulated Chinese mark. About 1750–55.

Three distinct styles of decoration are found upon the small dishes *a*, *b*, and *c*. That upon the Liverpool example is in Chinese style, and the border is a common one on Liverpool ware, although found also on Worcester and Lowestoft. It is probable that the specimen was made by Chaffers. Although fairly early, the flower-painting on the openwork Worcester basket is purely English—and should be compared with the more stylised Chinese flowers. The applied flowers on the outside of this basket are clearly visible. The style of the Chinese scene on the third dish is that of an artist whose work is frequently found on Worcester porcelain, and the border, similar to that on the basket, is the "pineapple" pattern which was also used at Caughley.

The similarity between the powder-blue plates is more marked in the photograph than in reality. Not only is the blue of the Caughley example (*e*) of a paler shade, and that of the Bow strong, and inclined to indigo, but the potting of the Worcester example (*d*) is superior to both the Caughley and the Bow, especially as regards the foot rim. It was at one time doubted whether plates of this type were in fact made at Caughley, but the presence of the impressed word SALOPIAN on the one illustrated is conclusive. Lowestoft examples were usually marked with a simpler, more artificial simulated Chinese mark, although unmarked specimens are common.

PLATE 2

a   b   c

d   e   f

II

PLATE 3

PLATE 3

VARIOUS FACTORIES

a WORCESTER MUG. Height, 2½ in. Open crescent mark. About 1760–75.

b WORCESTER MUG. Height, 2½ in. Hatched crescent mark. About 1770.

c CAUGHLEY MUG. Height, 4½ in. Hatched crescent mark. About 1775.

d LIVERPOOL MUG (Pennington's). Height, 2½ in. Unmarked. About 1760.

e WORCESTER MUG. Height, 2½ in. Hatched crescent mark. About 1775.

N.B. *b*, *c*, and *e* are transfer printed

Mugs of cylindrical shape were popular at all the three western factories. Examples of the work of the artist responsible for the decoration of the painted Worcester example (*a*) are fairly common, and are characterised by the unusual trees, a building with a top-heavy roof, and solid round clumps of weed, like cannon balls. Yet another style of tree-painting is seen on the Pennington's Liverpool mug (*d*), and the gnome-like Chinese figures are characteristic of the artist. This piece has a flat base, but another in my possession, similar in every other respect, has a narrow foot rim. The photograph does not show the pale duck-egg tone of the body, or the "sticky blue" used by the artist. The two small printed mugs (*b* and *e*), are examples of the two most common varieties of printed Chinese landscape; (*e*) especially was often used on tea and coffee services. The "parrot and vine" print on the large Caughley mug was engraved by Robert Hancock at Worcester, and was first used in overglaze enamels. Exactly similar mugs were made at Worcester.

at many English country mansions. Pictures painted by such artists as Boucher, Pillemont, and Watteau, in Chinese style, were copied on porcelain. It would seem that this Chinese influence, although more directly traceable to Sèvres, actually originated at the Meissen (Dresden) factory, since specimens affected by it were made there as early as 1725. The name "Chinese Chippendale", though strictly applicable to furniture influenced by this phenomenon, is sometimes used to describe these interesting "chinoiseries". They are truly fantastic by reason of the quaint mixture of Chinese and English idiom which is their outstanding feature, but they have an attraction of their own. They were more often printed than painted, chiefly at Worcester, Caughley, and Liverpool (Plate 43).

4. Meissen influence. More commonly known as Dresden, specimens from this factory followed the Chinese models as the inspiration of the English designers. The decoration copied was mainly floral, and both printed and painted wares were produced. Butterflies and other small insects were often included in the design (Plate 34). It will be noted that pieces bearing this style of decoration cannot belong to the very earliest period.

5. Decoration in English taste. By 1770 there was a tendency to depart from foreign influence, and to develop an English style. Thus English fruits and vegetables were made the subjects for decoration on domestic ware (Plate 34), and so were rural scenes such as milkmaids, haymakers, cattle, and landscapes (Plate 36). Sporting prints were popular, especially hunting, fishing, and shooting incidents. Pictures by famous artists were copied, an example of which is the "Rural Lovers" by Gainsborough.

6. Delft influence. The large amount of delft produced in the seventeenth and eighteenth centuries, both in England and on the Continent, had an appreciable and natural effect on porcelain decoration. Among pieces so influenced are those bearing initials and dates, a practice common on delft ware, usually on articles made for commemorative purposes such as marriage or Christmas gifts (Plate 41). At Lowestoft especially, a large amount of inscribed ware was produced, on which the potters strove to imitate the tone of blue and the delft glaze as well as the decoration. At Bristol also, where much delft

was produced, we find identical designs on both delft and porcelain. Indeed, Michael Edkins, a famous painter of Bristol delft and white opaque glass, decorated porcelain at the Redcliff Backs factory. Characteristic of his work are the moulded pieces painted with his gnome-like Chinese figures.

There, broadly speaking, we have the styles of decoration which we may expect to find on early blue and white porcelain. Practically every piece falls into one or other of the classes, and so a specimen may be dated according to its decoration, at all events as far as the earliest possible date for it is concerned, although naturally enough a popular pattern would be continued until its popularity waned, as witness the "Willow Pattern"!

Apart from decoration by means of colour, we must also consider the decorative value of moulding and applied moulded ornament. I have already mentioned that a partner in the Worcester firm was a silversmith, Bradley by name. In addition, Sprimont, manager of the Chelsea factory, was a member of the same trade, as were the Elers brothers, who made pottery at an earlier date. It was, therefore, inevitable that silver shapes should be copied, and pieces moulded in their likeness were produced at the early factories. Included among the moulded articles were sauce-boats, dishes, tea and coffee-pots, cream and butter-boats, plates, cups and saucers, baskets, and tureens, all richly moulded in exact silver style. Reserves formed in the moulding were decorated with Chinese scenes of figures, or with flowers, and with flower sprays in the bottoms, inside the lip or rim, scattered indiscriminately over the outside, often without any regard to the lines of the moulding. On many specimens moulded all over with floral ornament the only additional decoration was a slight border of leaves or diaper around the base and shoulder, or on the rim in the case of cups and saucers (Plates 25 and 44). One of the most delightful types of moulded ware is the perforated basket or dish. In such specimens the intention was to imitate basket or trellis-work, and moulded flowers were applied to the intersections on the outside, although this was not always the practice, particularly at Bow. Handles on such articles were often fashioned in the shape of twigs or cords (Plate 13). Unpierced basket patterns were common, sometimes with alternate

PLATE 4

VARIOUS FACTORIES

a LOWESTOFT PICKLE-TRAY. Diameter, $3\frac{3}{4}$ in. Workman's mark. About 1760–70.

b LONGTON HALL PICKLE-TRAY. Diameter, 4 in. Unmarked. About 1755.

c LOWESTOFT PICKLE-TRAY. Diameter, $2\frac{1}{2}$ in. Unmarked. About 1760.

d WORCESTER PICKLE-TRAY. Diameter, 3 in. Workman's mark. About 1760.

e CAUGHLEY PICKLE-TRAY. Diameter, $2\frac{1}{2}$ in. Capital S mark. About 1775.

f WORCESTER PICKLE-TRAY. Diameter, 3 in. Workman's mark. About 1760.

g LOWESTOFT PICKLE-TRAY. Diameter, $3\frac{3}{4}$ in. Workman's mark. About 1760–70.

N.B. *e* is transfer printed

Pickle-trays or sweetmeat-trays are among the daintiest of pieces, and recall to memory the days when neither pickles nor sweetmeats were plentiful! The Lowestoft examples (*a*, *c*, and *g*) are daintily decorated, and it will be noted that two of them bear workmen's marks. All three are painted with a pigment which is very granular in texture, and are made of a very white paste, showing a pale green translucency by transmitted light. The Longton Hall tray (*b*) shows very clearly the Longton "Littler blue", and also another characteristic mentioned in the text—that the edges appear to have been cut with a knife. The Caughley ivy-leaf tray is decorated with the "fisherman pattern", engraved by Thomas Turner, and very common on Salopian wares. The Worcester specimens both have the same decoration, which is an adaptation of the Japanese "partridge" pattern. The scallop shell was a favourite shape at Worcester, and was made in many sizes.

PLATE 4

a   e   c   g

b   d   f

PLATE 5

a

b

c

PLATE 5

VARIOUS FACTORIES

a   CAUGHLEY TEA-POT.   Height, 4 in.   Unmarked.   About 1775.

b   WORCESTER TEA-POT.   Height, 5 in.   Open crescent mark.   About 1760–70.

c   LOWESTOFT TEA-POT.   Height, 4 in.   Unmarked.   About 1760.

N.B.   *a* is transfer printed

Globular tea-pots are among the most pleasing shapes to be found in porcelain. The work of the artist who painted the "cannon ball" weeds is to be seen on the Worcester example, which should be compared with the Lowestoft one, which was clearly copied from it. The shape of the latter, it should be noted, is not so perfectly spherical as either of its companions. The cell diaper and fleur-de-lis border on the Caughley pot was used more than any other, almost invariably with some variety of Chinese scene.

sections of pierced work, particularly at Worcester. Applied moulded flowers are often found at the place of juncture of twig handles with the body (Plate 40). The knob or knap of tea and coffee-pot covers, cream-jug covers, and sucriers (sugar basins) was sometimes formed into the shape of a flower, either open or closed (Plates 5 and 40).

Reference to moulded wares would be incomplete without mention of what are commonly known as "cabbage leaf" jugs, moulded with overlapping cabbage leaves, sometimes with the lip in the form of a human bearded face (mask lip) and sometimes without any lip at all (Plates 27 and 31). Such jugs were made at Worcester, Caughley, and Lowestoft, and in size are found to vary from smaller sizes to enormous ones over a foot in height. I do not think the largest ones were intended as ewers, since I have never found a basin to match, but it is possible that they may have been intended for use as harvest jugs or "bell-ringers". They were both painted and printed, and are extremely decorative.

Among smaller wares are to be found tiny sweetmeat or pickle-trays in the shape of ivy leaves and scallop shells, spoons of various sorts, and large centre-pieces, tripartite, moulded in the form of scallop shells and raised on bases formed of beautifully fashioned shells of every variety and form. All types of gadrooned, scalloped, waved, crimped, and fluted edges were copied from Chinese models, as were certain baluster vases of bronze shape.* Moulded handles, often intricately scrolled, or fashioned in the form of serpents, dragons, or dolphins, were commonly used on sauce-boats and jugs (Plate 24) and, together with certain forms of cup handles, often afford valuable clues to identification.

It will perhaps be well here to repeat the warning that moulding in itself affords little certain proof of origin (except in a very few cases to which I shall draw special attention), even when fragments of such specimens or moulds have been unearthed on factory sites. Nothing was easier than to make plaster of Paris moulds of existing models, and it is certain that this was the common practice. For this reason it is advisable to examine the details of the moulding, since, although a well-used mould would be likely to lose its original sharpness of detail, a replica made in this manner would undoubtedly suffer from the same defect.

* See p. 172, note 5.

PLATE 6

BOW DISH. Length, 8 in. Marked numeral 1 in blue. About 1755–60.

An interesting piece painted with the "Image" pattern, mention of which is made in the memorandum book of John Bowcocke, the travelling manager of the factory, who wrote : "they must all be the bordered image, blue and pale as you please". The word "image" was used to signify "figure". As would be expected, the paste is very opaque except in the thin parts of the fluting, where a faint yellow translucency is visible by transmitted light. The glaze is slightly blued and is opalescent; the painting, in pale blue, is executed with great attention to detail and with a fine brush.

Chapter III

BOW BLUE AND WHITE PORCELAIN

THERE IS very little evidence, documentary or otherwise, on which to build a history of the Bow factory. It would appear that in the year 1744 an engraver and artist, Thomas Frye by name, sought the help of Edward Heylyn, a glass manufacturer of Bow, in a series of experiments with a view to the manufacture of porcelain. Heylyn was naturally the possessor of a kiln, and doubtless to the detriment of his legitimate business a period of experiment followed, which lasted until 1749, by which time his patience, and perhaps his capital, were exhausted. Frye thereupon sought the aid of two London merchants, Weatherby and Crowther, who by reason of their connection with the Chinese trade were probably interested in porcelain. Together they built a new factory on Chinese lines, which they named the "New Canton". This partnership was evidently successful, the merchants supplying the capital, and their manager, Frye, the experience and the brains, until a series of misfortunes brought the enterprise to a close. Weatherby died in 1762, and Crowther became bankrupt. Then followed a somewhat precarious period of hand-to-mouth existence until the factory closed in 1775–6, Duesbury of Derby removing everything of value to his own factory, as he had already done in the case of Chelsea (1770) and, probably, Longton Hall (1758).

The period of experiment referred to could not have resulted in any great amount of saleable ware. Doubtless, bearing in mind that Heylyn's experience and apparatus were those of a glass-maker, the paste and glaze would bear a strong resemblance to glass, although rendered milky or creamy by the addition of some form of clay, even in the case of the glaze, which would, therefore, resemble the perfectly transparent glaze of a later period. It may be presumed that any decoration attempted would most probably take the form of painting in blue, since, as will be seen later, Frye's new enterprise with his new

5   23

partners did not at first attempt any large-scale manufacture of any other style. There are no specimens which may be definitely identified.

With the new partnership Frye took out a patent for a body which he had by this time perfected. The important point to remember is that calcined or burnt bones were used in conjunction with flint or sand and pipe-clay, resulting in what is now known as a phosphatic or bone-ash paste. At the same time a lead glaze was used, glassy and transparent.

At some later period the paste was further changed by the addition of ground Oriental porcelain, with the intention of rendering it more pliable and at the same time capable of competing with its Worcester rival, which was able to withstand boiling water. It must be remembered, however, that in all probability experiment continued, and many modifications of the phosphatic paste may have been used although it was never given up, having proved itself to be (as Spode discovered later) a durable and economical material.

There can be no doubt that an enormous amount of blue and white was made at the New Canton factory. This is indicated by an advertisement in Aris's *Birmingham Gazette* for November 1753 which runs: "This is to give notice to all painters in the blue and white potting way and enamellers on china ware, that by applying at the counting-house at the China-House near Bow, they may meet with employment and proper encouragement according to their merit". It is significant also that on the opening of the factory commemorative pieces were made in the form of cylindrical inkstands, painted in blue, inscribed "Made at New Canton" and dated 1750. It would appear, as has already been mentioned, that Frye felt the effect of Worcester competition in the market for blue and white. Hurlbutt, in his *Bow Porcelain*, has pointed out that, whereas the Worcester paste was extremely suitable for the manufacture of rounded articles and not for plates and saucers, the characteristics of Frye's own body were exactly opposite, as a result of his addition of ground Oriental porcelain. This addition resulted in a paste of extreme strength, so that although a Bow plate may chip, it seldom cracks. Despite his endeavour Frye found it impossible to continue in competition with his rival, and about 1755 he practically discontinued blue painting in favour of polychrome

PLATE 7

a   *b*   *c*

d   *e*

PLATE 7

BOW

a SAUCE-BOAT. Length, 7½ in. Unmarked. About 1755–65.

b TEA-BOWL AND SAUCER. Unmarked. About 1755–65.

c TEA-POT. Height, 4 in. Unmarked. About 1755–65.

d SMALL MUG. Height, 3 in. Mark: Script capital G. About 1745.

e SAUCE-BOAT. Length, 7½ in. Unmarked. About 1755–65.

Except for the flower-painting on one of the sauce-boats (which is painted in the style of an enamel painter whose work is seen often on Bow porcelain), all the specimens illustrated here are decorated in the Chinese style. The handleless tea-cup and saucer has the typical Bow peony with its shaded petals, and a tree which I have not seen on any other make of porcelain. Miniature tea services were made at many factories, but Bow specimens are uncommon. This particular piece is painted in a very pale blue, with extensive use of washes, and a tree with horizontal boughs, upon which are short vertical branches. The small mug marked with a script capital G is an early piece, and the decoration is extremely elementary. It is interesting to note that a fragment with similar decoration was found on the site of the Bow factory (see Chap. XIV), The blue is most unusual, of poor quality, pale, and absolutely lifeless.

wares, employing many of the out-of-work Chelsea enamellers for the purpose.

Let us now consider the characteristics of the blue and white porcelain produced during the 1750–55 period. The paste was sometimes of greenish translucency owing to the admixture of cobalt in the paste to neutralise the creamy tone which was despised by those who had become accustomed to Oriental "Nankin" (blue and white) porcelain. At other times it was of a bluish-grey hue for the same reason. Tearings, half-moon or circular in shape, are of frequent occurrence, due to unmixed particles of clay in the paste. The glaze has a waxen appearance, is transparent and bluish, and is soft enough to be easily scratched. Excess of lead often caused brown discoloration due to decomposition, which is usually round the foot rim, and the presence of lead is also the cause of a certain amount of iridescence. Many specimens are disfigured by black specks, the result of faulty combustion in the kiln. Great weight and complete opacity in all but the thinnest parts are distinctive features of Bow porcelain; indeed, many plates may be mistaken for earthenware, although the decoration was always much more carefully executed than that to be found on the latter ware.

There are several important points to be noted in connection with the shapes of Bow specimens. Octagonal plates were much favoured, and an unusual foot rim, with no exterior wall, is commonly found on them. Yet another form of foot was sometimes used, rimless but slightly hollowed, and covered all over with glaze. Foot rims of cups and saucers were often very tiny, thin, and well modelled, or low and rounded. The glaze is often found to have accumulated inside the foot rim, where it has a bluish-grey colour. The foot rims of bowls sometimes bear spur marks.*

Many fine mugs, both bell-shaped and cylindrical, were made at Bow. The former have sturdy ring-shaped bases, and a characteristic of the latter is that the body swells out to a greater diameter at the base. Handles on cups and mugs often join the body horizontally instead of at an angle as at Worcester or Lowestoft, and a definite proof of Bow origin is a heart-shaped lower terminal to the handles of mugs and tea-pots (Plate 9).

* See p. 169, note 2.

28

Two tones of blue are to be found, the one extremely pale, the other peculiarly strong, almost an indigo-purple, which was used on later wares. The latter was used on the octagonal and round powder-blue plates mentioned in an earlier chapter, which are distinguishable from the Worcester variety by the inferior finish of the foot rim, and from the Lowestoft by the superior tone of blue and the different glaze. The use of the peony in decoration, with petals shaded in parallel lines, is frequently encountered (Plates 8 and 9). Yet another style of decoration often found on Bow blue and white is the so-called "Image" pattern already referred to, whose Bow origin is proved by a reference to it in the papers of John Bowcocke, who was the manager of the Frye-Heylyn partnership, and by the discovery of a fragment of a piece so decorated on the site of the Bow factory.* The "Jumping Boy" pattern was also a favourite subject, and is peculiarly effective on certain hexagonal and octagonal cups and saucers which were extensively copied at Liverpool (Plate 45). The Bow variety usually bears a simulated Chinese four-character mark. Among specimens decorated in Chinese style a distinctive form of tree is common, with perfectly perpendicular horizontal trunk or trunks, branches at right angles, and hanging willow sprays in bunches of four (Plate 7). Mention has already been made of specimens bearing the Chinese Dragon, clouds, and lightning, at Worcester, Caughley, and Bow; it will be found that Bow pieces are never so neatly drawn as those of Worcester, and that the blue is usually much run.

As far as printed decoration is concerned, although John Bowcocke mentions "blue printed mugs, 5/–", so far as I am aware no specimens of Bow printed in underglaze blue have been identified, although it is well known that overglaze printing in black, puce, and red was carried on.

The marks found on Bow porcelain have been the subject of much controversy in the past. An example of this was the attribution to Bow of a TF monogram, which was commonly thought to represent the initials of the proprietor. That this was not so has been proved by its presence on an undoubted Worcester tureen in the Dyson Perrins Collection, which bears this mark, as do many other pieces of the

* See Appendix, p. 176, note 12.

PLATE 8

BOW

SAUCE-BOAT.   Length 9 in.   Unmarked.   About 1755–60.

There are many silver sauce-boats in existence which may well have served as model for this unusually large and heavy specimen. The paste is white, and the piece is so thickly potted that its yellowish translucency is visible only in the thinnest parts. The glaze has decomposed around the base, resulting in brown patches. The decoration, in pale blue, is typical, and includes the peony and the palm-like trees seen on the mug in Plate 7. A similar sauce-boat in the South Kensington Museum has an incised planet mark.

PLATE 8

PLATE 9

PLATE 9

BOW

MUG. Height, 6 in. Unmarked. About 1755–65.

A very lovely Bow mug, of rare pattern and pleasing shape. Although heavy and thickly potted, there is no clumsiness in the workmanship. The paste is slightly blued, giving a slight green tinge to the translucency, which is visible only in the centre of the base and near the rim. A very important fact is that the lower terminal of the handle is heart-shaped, a feature peculiar to Bow. The peony and the Chinese border ("ch'ing t'i pai hua") are painted in strong vivid blue. Similar borders are to be found on Worcester pieces.

same origin. It is actually an English version of a Chinese character signifying "jade". There is also a smaller version of the same mark, which is included among the "workmen's marks" at the end of this book. Such marks are found on Worcester and Bow porcelain, and, to a much less extent, on Lowestoft. No better explanation than that they were in fact the signatures of the artists has ever been proffered, and as the presence of the same mark on different patterns is common they can have no reference to a pattern book. The simulated Chinese marks commonly found on Bow powder-blue specimens are in the majority of cases distinguishable from the somewhat similar Worcester mark by the fact that the latter generally incorporates several unmistakable script W's. The script capital G sometimes found would appear to denote very early experimental pieces, since all the ware which I have examined bearing that mark is characterised by elementary workmanship and decoration (Plate 7).

Chapter IV

CHELSEA BLUE AND WHITE PORCELAIN

THERE IS little doubt that porcelain was first made at the "Chelsea Porcelaine Manufacture" between the years 1740 and 1743; the evidence for this date being the existence of a class of small jugs, known as the "goat and bee" jugs, incised with the word "Chelsea", the date 1743 or 1745, and a triangle. The jugs themselves, copied from a silver model, are modelled in the form of a vessel resting upon two goats, with a twig handle and, usually, a bee under the lip.

The jugs bearing the date 1745 have been recognised as valuable documentary evidence for many years, but the discovery of a jug of undoubted authenticity bearing the earlier date of 1743, reported by Dr. F. Severne Mackenna in *Apollo*, December 1944, antedates the founding of the factory by several years, because the quality and workmanship are such that the factory must have been in existence some years previous to the actual date incised on the base of the jug in question.

The problem then arises—who was the founder of the factory responsible for the manufacture of these early pieces? There is abundant evidence to show that Nicholas Sprimont (*b.* 1716, *d.* 1771), a silversmith of Huguenot extraction, was connected with the factory from its earliest days; but, in addition, the fact that he was helped by a technician with some knowledge of porcelain making, is proved by his reference in an appeal for heavier duties on imported Meissen porcelain to "a casual acquaintance with a chymist who had some knowledge that way", which had led him to commence manufacture. Tradition has long named Charles Gouyn, a fellow silversmith, as this unknown "chymist", although there was little supporting evidence save a reference to him as "late Proprietor and Chief Manager of the Chelsea-House" which appeared in the Press in 1750. Obviously, this

6

PLATE 10

CHELSEA

HEXAGONAL BOWL.　　Height, 2⅜ in.　　Diameter, 2⅝ in.　　Unmarked.
About 1750.

This interesting specimen is proof that, despite its extreme rarity, Chelsea blue and white can nevertheless be found. The paste resembles a milk-white glass, into which the blue decoration has sunk, so that it is visible on the inside. The glaze is thin and vitreous, of milky texture and marred inside the bottom of the bowl by black spots and sand. The foot rim is low, rounded, and unground. By transmitted light the paste is greenish, with small flecks of greater translucency. The painting is careful, and is executed in a good vivid blue, which has formed blobs in the flower centres over which the glaze failed to adhere. The piece is probably early, belonging to the period when the body was similar to that used at Bow.

PLATE 10

date is too late to be of any great value when the question of the founding of the factory is under consideration.

On the other hand, Professor Church, in the Victoria and Albert Museum *Guide to English Porcelain*, published in 1911, suggested Thomas Briand as the predecessor of Gouyn (who it is known worked as a silversmith from 1737 until his death in 1784) as Sprimont's partner; a suggestion which is upheld by other documentary evidence. Thus, at a meeting of the Royal Society in February 1743 the members were addressed by a Mr. Bryant (Briand?) who showed "several specimens of a sort of fine white ware, made here by himself from natural materials of our own country", and a later record in the Journal of the Society refers to him as Thomas Briand. It would appear most probable that this was the same Thomas Briand who, according to Dr. Bellamy Gardner, was a modeller for the Bristol factory many years later. Again, the marked similarity between St. Cloud porcelain and early Chelsea, both as regards paste and style of modelling, would seem to suggest that Briand, who like Sprimont was a Huguenot, may have had experience at the former factory. To sum up, therefore, the logical conclusion is that Briand, successful in his experiments, was joined by Sprimont in order to found the factory, and that, at some later date, he was superseded by Charles Gouyn, who became a sleeping partner, and took but little practical part in the business.

In the year 1769 Sprimont, who for some time seems to have been in poor health and whose finances were at a low ebb, sold his factory to a James Cox, who in turn sold it to William Duesbury and John Heath of Derby, after which time the products of the firm were known as Chelsea-Derby. Specimens produced during this period are difficult to identify as the work of either factory and show the characteristics of both.

Because of the fact that Chelsea porcelain was usually marked, it is not difficult to trace the development of the ware, although in common with the other early factories this was inevitably the result of experiment with many different pastes. The earliest porcelain was akin to Bow, resembling a heavy milk-white glass, with flecks of a greater translucency (known as Chelsea "moons") revealed by artificial light in an otherwise yellowish paste. The glaze was extremely soft, of thin, vitreous, milky texture, very easily scratched, and often marred by dark spots, caused by its sinking into the paste. Foot rims were often ground flat and so are found to be soft and smooth to the touch. The bottoms of plates and dishes often show three unglazed patches or spots which were made by the tripods on which the pieces were supported in the glost oven.

About 1750 an improvement (as far as durability was concerned) was made in the paste, which became harder and cold in appearance, often thick, but never clumsy. "Moons" were still present, but the glaze was smooth and even and never crazed, while there were no more dark spots.

Bone ash was incorporated in the body at a later date, probably about 1759, with a view to a decrease of wasters in the kiln. At the same time a thicker, fuller, more shining glaze was adopted, which, however, was apt to craze, and tended to collect in greenish pools around the bases of plates or dishes, making it even more imperative to grind the foot rims.

It has never been satisfactorily explained why blue and white was never popular at Chelsea. It is obvious that a great popular demand existed for that type of ware, a fact which was used to advantage by every other factory. Alone among them all, the Chelsea proprietors did not avail themselves of a golden opportunity. I think the probability is that the neglect of underglaze blue painting was due in a large degree to the enterprise of the factory, which clearly set out to imitate the forms and decoration of the Oriental, Meissen, and Sèvres. In this the proprietors were doubtless helped by the existence in Chelsea of a flourishing artists' colony (which included such men as Sir James Thornhill, Askew, Barton, Gauron, Dyer, Hall, and Franz de Paula) and by the probable easier acquisition of colour materials in bulk. That their policy was in any way due to contempt of blue and white ware I do not for a moment believe, although it is perhaps true that they strove to cater for a small and select clientèle who were attracted by the dainty toys and graceful figures which they made so well in the fashionable French style. Had they not chosen to specialise in polychrome wares there would have been no lack of fine Oriental models in blue and white, graceful in form, splendid in decoration, and in the highest taste.

However that may be, the only reference to its production is to be found in a Sale Catalogue of 1776, sponsored by the factory, when the following pieces of Chelsea porcelain were offered :—

"Two small blue and white sallad dishes."
"Two large blue and white open-worked dishes."

At the present moment very few specimens have been identified, the only well-authenticated museum pieces being as follows :—

1. A soup-plate, painted with two mythical Chinese birds, in a rocky landscape with trees. On the rim is a diaper border interrupted by five panels enclosing flowers. The edge is lobed. The piece is marked with an anchor in underglaze blue. (In the Schreiber Collection.)

2. An octagonal cup and saucer painted with a river scene in Chinese style, with islands and temples, and a man fishing from the bank in the foreground, near which is a boat, with a man at the oars. Both specimens have the blue anchor mark.

Needless to say, in the light of what has already been said, under-glaze blue transfer printing was never used at Chelsea; indeed, it is doubtful whether printing of any sort was done, since the very few pieces of Chelsea so decorated may well have been printed at Battersea.

The rarity of Chelsea blue and white need not deter the collector from hoping that a piece of it may one day come into his possession as, indeed, one did recently into mine (Plate 10). Indeed, it may be that there are specimens of it now wrongly labelled, which may at some future date prove to be Chelsea, with a resultant upheaval in many cabinets! Let me conclude this (to the blue and white collector, at any rate) unsatisfying chapter by saying that if such a piece *does* come his way, he may expect it to be not so creamy as Worcester, or so green as Lowestoft, or so hard as Bow. The potting will probably be coarser than any, but the paste much whiter. The glaze will be thick, like a coat of glass, and there may be tears or pools of it in the centre of the base.

Chapter V

LOWESTOFT BLUE AND WHITE PORCELAIN

No OTHER English porcelain has been so misunderstood as Lowestoft. Indeed, even at the present day there are many dealers and collectors who by the word Lowestoft understand a class of hard paste Chinese porcelain painted with pink roses and with applied white clay ornamentation. Sometimes they call it "Chinese Lowestoft". True, much polychrome Lowestoft is decorated with pink roses, but there the resemblance ends. For our purpose it is sufficient to say that the mistake arose through an error in an early edition of *Marks and Monograms on Pottery and Porcelain* by Chaffers. In fact, no hard paste was ever made at Lowestoft, neither was Chinese porcelain decorated there to any considerable extent.

According to Gillingham, in his book *An Historical Account of the Ancient Town of Lowestoft*, which was published in 1790, a factory was founded in the year 1757 by Messrs. Walker, Aldred, Richman, and Robert Browne. The latter is reputed to have worked at the Bow factory, and to have brought the secret to Lowestoft, and certain it is that the pastes are very similar, both being of bone-ash composition. The factory finally closed in 1802, and this long life, despite the fact that the premises were very modest, accounts for the very large quantity of Lowestoft porcelain in existence. Such a long life of a small factory in the face of considerable opposition on the part of the larger and richer factories was due solely to the fact that ambitious ventures were avoided and domestic needs were catered for.

The porcelain made at Lowestoft was of a creamy hue, with a thick blued glaze which bubbled on the bottoms of cups and saucers, and lay thickly inside the foot rim and at such places as the junctions of handles, etc. In contrast to any other porcelains the whole of the article was covered by the glaze, even to the insides of pot lids, which, be it noted, were usually left unglazed at Worcester and Caughley. Bases were often

PLATE II

LOWESTOFT COFFEE-POT. Height, 9¼ in. Unmarked. About 1760.

The provenance of this specimen is proved by the tone of the brilliant powder-blue ground and the blurred outlines of the reserves and of the painting of the landscapes and flowers, due to the running of the glaze. The paste is much blued, and the interior of pot and cover disfigured with smears and spots of blue pigment.

PLATE 12

a   b   c

d

PLATE 12

LOWESTOFT

a   TEA-BOWL AND SAUCER.   Diameter (saucer), 4½ in.   Unmarked.
     About 1760–70.

b   SAUCE-BOAT.   Length, 6 in.   Unmarked.   About 1760–70.

c   TEA-BOWL AND SAUCER.   Unmarked.   About 1760–70.

d   SAUCE-BOAT.   Length, 8 in.   Unmarked.   About 1760–70.
          N.B.   *d* has transfer-printed flowers, the border painted

Typical pieces of Lowestoft. The moulded cup and saucer are interesting because they belong to a class whose provenance is proved by the discovery of
moulds in the old factory buildings. A similar cup and saucer in the Schreiber
Collection has the initials "I.H." and the date 1764 introduced in the moulding.
These moulded pieces are usually made of a very white paste, which appears
pale yellow by transmitted light. The Chinese scene on the other cup and saucer,
which has the "duck-egg blue" paste and greenish translucency, is commonly
found on Lowestoft porcelain, and its characteristics should be noted. Among
the several shapes of sauce-boat made at Lowestoft, that represented by the
two examples pictured here is the most common, and was made in several
mouldings. "*b*" is painted, the other printed, save for the border, which is a
painted "pineapple" pattern. The beautiful moulding of this specimen should
be examined. One of the most outstanding features of Lowestoft blue and white
painting and printing, the hesitant appearance of the drawing (or engraving),
can be seen in these pieces.

ground level. As with other early factories, the blueing of the glaze was probably intentional and is artistically good, although certain specimens, notably moulded ones, were covered with a clear glaze which shows the creamy paste to excellent advantage, and which is more pleasing to modern eyes than the more typical "duck-egg blue" usually characteristic of Lowestoft blue and white. Most specimens, like Bow, were heavy for their size, and were often disfigured by black or blue spots, and sanded. A further likeness to Bow is noticeable in that the tone of blue and the appearance of the surface bear strong resemblance to the earlier Dutch delft.

Documentary evidence as to what is and what is not Lowestoft is provided by numerous pieces inscribed "A Trifle from Lowestoft", among which are tea-poys and inkstands. Although it must be acknowledged that there is no actual proof that these pieces were in fact made at Lowestoft, their resemblance as far as paste and glaze is concerned to certain plates decorated with powder-blue and bearing views of the town in irregularly shaped reserves is so strong as to be conclusive. A fortunate occurrence some years ago was the discovery on the site of the old factory of a considerable number of plaster moulds and fragments of porcelain. That this discovery was of great value to the collector will be realised from a perusal of the following list of some of the types of ware found. An artichoke butter-boat, with the feet formed of raised leaf decoration; knife-handles, embossed and plain; toy tea-cups decorated in blue, and portions of baskets, butter-boats, and tea-pots; covers for tea and coffee-pots, ribbed, plain, and with raised flowers or medallions; tea-pot stands, bases of mugs, cups, and saucers (many bearing Chinese landscapes in blue), spouts, and portions of bowls.

Among the types of ware thus identified the moulded specimens are very interesting. They are daintily made, charming, and among the loveliest of English porcelains. There is indeed a toy-like quality about much Lowestoft which one might expect from a factory which made souvenir pieces. The earliest tea-cups, for example, were only $2\frac{15}{16}$ in. in diameter, and in addition many miniature services were made. Both this earlier type of tiny cup and saucer and the later and larger ones were almost invariably handleless, although moulded cups were sometimes handled. Outstanding among the moulded wares were tea services in which round medallions were reserved in the all-over moulding, to be decorated later with tiny Chinese landscapes, and a simple diaper border added to the edges. A cup and saucer of this class in the Victoria and Albert Museum bears in addition the date 1764 introduced into the moulding (Plate 12). Moulded sauce-boats were similar in design and moulding to those made at Worcester and Bow, and large quantities were produced (Plate 12). As shown by the fragments found on the site, open-work baskets with applied flowers at the intersections were much favoured, as was the class of jug known as "cabbage leaf", either with or without the mask lip. The flower knob on tea-pot covers so common on Worcester articles was often used, but whereas the Worcester flower was usually half or fully open, the Lowestoft flower is usually closed. The insides of tea-pots often bear quite distinct ridges or rings similar to those found inside the hard paste pots and bowls made at Bristol and Plymouth.

In common with Liverpool, much Lowestoft blue and white has been mistakenly attributed to Worcester. The workmanship, however, is usually much inferior (it is said that most of the painting was done by women!) and the tone of blue is commonly dark, often with a distinct greyish tinge, although violet-toned blue was also used on occasion. Some excuse, of course, can be found for this mistaken attribution by the fact that many of the commoner patterns used at Worcester (and indeed at other factories) were copied. Otherwise the blue and white Lowestoft decoration was almost entirely copied from Chinese models, including in particular the familiar subjects of Chinese houses, gnarled tree trunks or roots, decorative palings, plants with enormous flowers, water scenes with bridges, islets, clumps of rushes or weeds, and boats. A characteristic which is not found to the same extent on the wares of any other factory is the addition of a central decoration on the inside of every cup or bowl, the subject often bearing no relation to that used on the outside (Plate 12). Not to be found on any other blue and white porcelain, also, are the dashes of blue on either side of the lower terminals of the handles of jugs, etc. Mention has already been made of the souvenir specimens. In addition to these, inkpots were made bearing names and dates (in all probability intended for the commemoration of such events as weddings and

7

christenings), mugs bearing inn signs or landlords' names, and punch-bowls with pictures of ships together with the names of their captains. Dated specimens seem to cover the years 1761–96. Such pieces as these speak eloquently of the English life of the period, and are fitting products of a factory which was content with a purely local trade and did not scorn to make articles to individual requirements. Powder-blue plates of the type already described as made at Worcester, Bow, and Caughley, in addition to those bearing Lowestoft views, were produced, but the blue is neither vivid nor strong, and the potting is inferior. Moreover, they were seldom marked. A point to be noted, however, is that many Lowestoft powder-blue plates do not have the usual fan-shaped and round reserves which are usually associated with this type of ware. Instead, the reserves are irregularly shaped, almost flat at the base, and with three curves at the top. Not only were plates decorated in the powder-blue styles, but also bowls, tea and coffee-pots, and tea-poys (Plate 11). Birth tablets were made at Lowestoft; small round discs upon which were inscribed the names and dates of birth of the children for whom they were made. I do not think they were ever made at any other factory.

Transfer printing was practised at Lowestoft on a small scale, and specimens so decorated may be identified by the spidery appearance of the prints, which were usually floral in conception. It is often diffi-cult to decide whether, in fact, the design is printed or painted, so fine are the lines and so natural the flowers. The printing is usually com-bined with painting, especially when diaper borders are employed, in which case the design is printed and the border painted or, more rarely, *vice versa* (Plate 12). No transfer printed pieces were found among the excavated fragments already mentioned, but these did include pieces of unglazed ware similar to those just discussed, and also to a very rare class of pieces decorated in "willow pattern" style.

Chapter VI

DERBY BLUE AND WHITE PORCELAIN

DERBY, WITH Worcester, shares the distinction of having made porcelain from the middle of the eighteenth century to the present day, and, with that factory, has always been famed for the excellence of its products. The exact date of the founding of the factory is unknown, although there is a tradition, based on the somewhat unreliable evidence of an old workman, that porcelain was made as early as 1745. Be that as it may, there are in existence pieces bearing the date 1750. An agreement dated January 1st, 1756, between John Heath, Andrew Planché, "china maker", and William Duesbury of Longton, "enamellor", for the purpose of a partnership "in the Art of Making English China" does nothing to bridge the gap of the intervening six years, and it can only be assumed that porcelain was indeed made during that period. A little later, in December of the same year, the *Public Advertiser* contained an advertisement of a London sale "by Order of the Proprietors of the Derby Porcelain Manufactory", which was followed in 1757 and 1758 by similar notices. It is interesting at this point to note that it was in the year 1757 that Duesbury is reputed to have purchased the Longton Hall factory and to have transferred a number of the workmen to Derby, with, we may suppose, some influence on Derby methods of production. In 1770 Duesbury likewise purchased the Chelsea factory, and, in 1776, that situated at Bow.

Derby blue and white is extremely rare, indeed, early Derby porcelain of any description was unidentified until Mr. Bernard Rackham found certain characteristics which tallied with those of later and known Derby specimens. Chief among these characteristics was the presence of three or four dark unglazed patches on the backs of specimens, which were caused by the pads of clay (used instead of the more usual stilts or tripods) upon which they rested in the glazing (or glost)

PLATE 13

DERBY

a BASKET. Length, 10 in. Unmarked. About 1760.

b COFFEE-CUP. Height, 2 in. Unmarked. About 1760.

This is a basket of the type fully described in the text. The photograph does not show the warping of the weakened sides, despite which fault the piece is really beautiful, with its white paste, delicate applied flowers to outside and handle terminals, and reticent decoration. The "fish-roe" diaper border is most uncommon. The very pale blue with which the decoration is carried out, although weak, is nevertheless effective. A feature shared by much Derby decorated with the pale blue is that the lines of the drawing appear to have been drawn with a pen, rather than with a brush. The coffee-cup is pictured by reason of its shape, which is peculiar to Derby, and to show the rather unusual form of decoration —the use of small disconnected motifs rather than a picture or pattern. The paste and the rather matt surfaced glaze are similar to those of the basket, but the glaze is disfigured with black specks near the base, clearly shown in the photograph.

PLATE 13

a

b

PLATE 14

PLATE 14

DERBY

PLATE. Diameter, 9½ in. Unmarked. About 1775.

A very beautiful and unusual plate. It is probably an accurate copy of a Chinese piece, and among the decoration may be seen the dragon, clouds, bats, lightning, and, in the centre, the symbol "shou" signifying longevity. It is interesting to note that the back of the plate is almost as decorative as the face. The paste is yellow by transmitted light, and the glaze, which is badly crazed all over, is nevertheless beautifully clear, soft, and glistening. The blue is pale but of excellent quality.

kiln.* The identification of the blue and white products of the factory however, was not completed until some ten years ago, when it came about in the following way. Mr. William King, in his well-known book on Chelsea porcelain, illustrated a plate as being of Chelsea manufacture. This attribution was doubted by Mr. Honey, who later described a dish in the Terry Collection, possessing similar characteristics to the plate, as being in his opinion of Derby origin. Mr. Frank Tilley, at the sale of the collection, purchased several pieces of the same class, including the dish, and succeeded in acquiring from another source a sauce-boat and a basket by the same painter and with, again, very similar characteristics. None was of Chelsea paste, but all had the "patch marks". Mr. Tilley gradually accumulated a small collection of pieces of this class and came to the conclusion that they were in fact early Derby; first, because they could not, on the evidence of paste and glaze, be Chelsea; secondly, that they were obviously too early (apart from other considerations) to be Chelsea-Derby; and lastly, they all had the typical Derby patch marks. In this conclusion Mr. Honey unhesitatingly concurred.

Now to consider the appearance of the specimens belonging to this class. The paste has a greenish translucency by artificial light, and has Chelsea-like moons. It is extremely dense, almost opaque, except in its thinnest parts. The glaze on some pieces is very shiny, but on others has very little gloss, possessing almost a matt surface, especially on the bottoms of articles, inside the foot rim. There are black spots and tiny dark pin-pricks over the whole of the surface. Many pieces are misshapen, especially in the case of pierced baskets and plates, which seem to have been a feature of the period. Such baskets are oval, with wavy rims and pierced sides, applied moulded flowers on the outside of the intersections, and double, twisted, rope-like handles with clusters of applied flowers at their terminals (Plate 13). The foot rims are ground level. In the case of the plates the applied flowers are found on the upper surface of the intersections. Coffee-cups have moulded handles with knobs below the upper and lower terminals, parallel sides, and flat bases with no foot rim (Plate 13).

It is a matter of extreme importance that the two types of glaze

* See p. 169, note 2.

mentioned have their exact counterparts on specimens of Longton Hall. I believe that many supposed pieces of Longton are in fact Derby. On this assumption it seems reasonable to suppose that the production of blue and white at Derby dated from the purchase of the Longton factory by Duesbury in 1757, and the ensuing migration of its workmen to his factory. Certainly by far the greater part of Longton production was decorated in blue, which was used in underglaze form even in conjunction with overglaze enamels.

The blue used in the decoration was of two kinds. One was a strong violet blue, running into blobs when used in any quantity, while the other was much paler, of a delicate sky-blue tone. In addition, whereas painting in the former pigment was executed in thick bold brush strokes, the latter was sparingly used with a hesitant brush, but with remarkable clarity and careful draughtsmanship. On larger pieces, such as the baskets and plates already described, the favourite subjects were landscapes and water scenes in Chinese style, with tree foliage formed of clusters of small filled-in circles. Undergrowth was represented by clumps of curved lines. Water was shown by parallel lines superimposed on washes of very pale blue. Fish-roe diaper was a popular form of border decoration. On smaller articles such as cups and saucers the surface was well covered with small detached motifs, among which are found "Long Elizas" with peculiarly large heads, tiny feet raised on tip-toe, and simpering expressions (Plate 13). Basket handles and moulded foot rims were commonly painted in a wash of blue which has a strong family likeness to the blue used at Longton Hall by Littler.

After the purchase of the Chelsea factory in 1770, blue and white of a superior quality was made at Derby, with the same greenish translucency, but beautifully white and clean in appearance, the glaze colourless and even, bright, and lustrous. The blue became stronger, but possessed a granular appearance similar almost to fine powder-blue. Extremely intricate brocades were a feature of the decoration, especially on the outsides of sauce-boats, which were often of unusually large size (Plate 15). The lower edges of such borders were skilfully blended with gracefully drawn flowers and leaves. Indeed, the result of the marrying of the elegance of Chelsea to the workmanship of

PLATE 15
CHELSEA-DERBY

SAUCE-BOAT.   Length 9 in.   Mark: blue cross on handle.   About 1770.

No photograph could do justice to the clear white paste, colourless glaze, brilliant blue, and perfect potting of this Chelsea-Derby specimen. The adaptation of Chinese brocade patterns is seen at its best, and the landscape in the bottom is beautifully drawn. The mark, a blue cross, is very rare, and is placed on the handle. Similar sauce-boats were made both at Chelsea and at Derby (after the purchase of the Chelsea factory by Duesbury), but were usually decorated in polychrome.

Derby resulted in blue and white ware which is almost as good as Worcester.

No mention has been made of overglaze blue printing at Derby. It was never adopted on a large scale. The manager of the Worcester printing department, Richard Holdship, left that factory in 1759 to join Duesbury, and attempted shortly afterwards to introduce blue printing, but although there are several specimens in existence bearing the word DERBY and an anchor (the rebus of Holdship), it is evident from the quality of the printing upon them that the Derby paste was in some way unsuitable for the process, which was discontinued.

Chapter VII

LONGTON HALL BLUE AND WHITE PORCELAIN

LONGTON HALL stands alone among the early English soft paste porcelains as the only one to be produced in Staffordshire, a county now world famous for its potteries and for the enormous amount of fine porcelain produced every year in its innumerable kilns. If not for the excellence of its ware, therefore, it is worthy of due consideration by reason of the pioneer nature of its history.

William Littler was a potter descended from a long line of potters, and in the year 1745 he commenced business on his own account as a manufacturer of salt-glazed earthenware in a small kiln at Brownhills near Burslem, which had been left to him by his father, a fact which was to have considerable influence upon the style of his later production of porcelain. Whether he actually made porcelain there is doubtful, although there is a tradition that he did so. In 1750, having failed to make a success of his undertaking, he moved to Longton Hall, a mansion near Stoke-on-Trent, and in 1752 there appeared an advertisement in the *Birmingham Gazette* of the "Porcelain or China Ware" which was produced by "William Littler & Co. at Longton Hall near Newcastle", the first of a series of such advertisements spaced over a period of six years. Mr. Nightingale, who was responsible for the discovery of the advertisements, has made the suggestion that during the latter part of this period Littler received the financial aid of Duesbury of Derby, and there is certainly much evidence to support his theory. Mr. Frank Jessop, a great-grandson of Duesbury, wrote in a letter that "Mr. William Duesbury . . . was the proprietor of works at Chelsea, Bow, Longton, and Derby". We have already read of the deed which was made in 1756 between John Heath, Planché, and "William Duesbury of Longton, enamellor", and in December, 1756, the newly established Derby factory was able to advertise the sale of a "curious collection of fine figures, jars, sauce-boats, services for dessert, and a great variety of other useful and ornamental porcelain", to be followed in May 1757, by a further sale of "a large variety of the Derby or second Dresden". As Mrs. Willoughby Hodgson has pointed out, it would seem that such a large stock must have been brought from some other factory; it could scarcely have been produced at a factory which had been in existence for a period of months. The similarity between Longton Hall and Derby blue and white which I have already pointed out is yet further support for this theory of a Littler-Duesbury alliance. The Derby factory established, and able fully to supply the needs of its customers, Duesbury finally bought up Littler's business, auctioned off all remaining wares on the spot, and transferred the skilled workmen to his own factory at Derby.

There is much contemporary evidence to show that Littler succeeded in making fine porcelain. Thus we read of its "great lightness and beauty", and that "the perfection to which porcelain is arrived is due to William Littler of Longton Hall". There exist very few specimens, and those generally figures, which live up to such a fine reputation. These few are flawless, tasteful, and cleanly finished, but the domestic wares are usually heavy, roughly potted, and often flawed, while the ornamental pieces are often overdecorated. However, the lack of perfection as judged by modern standards, and indeed as compared with the products of Worcester or Bow, is outweighed by the historical interest which must be felt in this courageous forerunner of the Staffordshire potteries.

Littler produced a great variety of wares. Among them, as listed in the sale advertisements were dishes and plates, tea and coffee equipages, dessert services, essence-pots, images, flowers, vases, fine blue and white ribbed, fluted, and octagonal chocolate-cups and saucers, tea-sets, tureens, jars and beakers, open-work baskets and plates, mugs, coffee-cans, punch-bowls, sauce-boats, leaf basins and plates, melons, cauli-flowers, epergnes, and fine figures.

The paste used by Littler was described by Staffordshire historians as a frit composition, and known specimens of Longton Hall exhibit characteristics appropriate to such a paste. Thus we find it to be hard-

61

PLATE 16

LONGTON HALL

a MUG. Height, 6 in. Unmarked. About 1755.
b and *c* TEA-CUPS. Height, 3 in. and 2¼ in. Unmarked. About 1755.

The two qualities of Longton Hall porcelain are shown in these photographs. Representative of the heavier, clumsily potted ware, the mug belongs to a class which at one time was thought to be a product of the Musselburgh (Scotland) factory. In this specimen an extensive fire crack is partly hidden by the handle. There is no blueing of the paste; the glaze has the appearance of candle fat, especially where it has run into pools on the unglazed, flat base; and the entire surface is marred by black specks. The cups, although appearing to be made of the same body, showing yellow by transmitted light, are thinly potted, and covered with a very glossy glaze (note the reflection of the handle). The running of the glaze has resulted in a rim of glaze around the base of the handled cup, and in distortion of the slanting blue panels. The streaky nature of the Littler blue is clearly shown.

PLATE 16

a

b   *c*

PLATE 17

PLATE 17

LONGTON HALL

TEA-BOWL AND SAUCER.   Diameter (saucer), 5 in.   About 1755–60.

Pieces belonging to the class of ware mentioned in the text. The painting is carried out in red, yellow, and blue. The border is similar to that on the tea-pot shown in Plate 43, and was probably printed by Zachariah Barnes at his Liverpool factory.

looking, heavy, and glassy, somewhat similar to Bow, and with a greyish tone. Two sorts of glaze appear to have been used, the one with a surface like candle grease, with an almost matt surface, the other very shiny and more blued. By artificial light there is a greenish translucency, although specimens showing dirty yellow may be found. Like Bow, the paste is almost opaque in the thicker parts. A curious granulated effect is sometimes noticeable, almost as though a powder were in suspension in the paste. Chelsea-like moons are often present.

In general the potting was clumsy and heavy, especially in larger pieces, with frequent fire cracks, often partly hidden by the handle in the case of mugs, etc., covered by decoration, or clumsily filled in. Bases were frequently flat and unfinished, with an exceedingly rough biscuit surface disfigured near the edge by blobs of run glaze, often impregnated with blue. Where glaze meets foot there is often a ridge of scummy glaze, discoloured or heavily blued.

Much use was made of moulding, as would be expected from Littler, who had been a manufacturer of salt-glazed ware which relied so much upon moulding for its decoration. Thus we find basins, dessert dishes, pickle-trays and the like with overlapping leaf moulding, or moulded into the shape of a single leaf, while around the bases of jugs, tea-pots, etc., there is often a pattern of similar overlapping leaves. It will be noted that this usual form of Longton moulding greatly differs from the moulding found on other porcelains, which was derived from the shapes of silver articles. A class of large, clumsily potted mugs, much warped in the firing, moulded with vertical reeding and with medallions on either side, is now known to be of Longton manufacture (Plate 16). Such mugs were at one time attributed to Musselburgh, a Scottish factory. They have, in common with many jugs, moulded handles of a form peculiar to Longton Hall. A characteristic of certain small leaf-shaped pickle-trays, many of which are unusually thin and well potted, is that they are supported upon three short conical feet. Their serrated edges often have the appearance of having been cut with a knife, although they are moulded pieces (Plate 4).

The decoration of Littler's blue and white is almost invariably elementary both in conception and in execution, and the blue used is unknown on any other porcelain. It was an invention of William

66

Littler, and is remarkably vivid and streaky, never even. It is probable that this was intentional and that the colour was laid on with a rag, so that it is often thinner on raised parts of the moulding, although thickly applied. Indeed, a border of it is perceptible to the touch, and always ran with the glaze, so that the flower painting and Chinese scenes used to decorate the insides of small trays and such-like articles are always blurred and indistinct (Plate 4). Broad diagonal panels of blue, which were commonly used to decorate the outsides of tea-cups and bowls, are seldom well shaped, owing to the vertical running of the glaze and consequently of the colour (Plate 16). Despite these shortcomings, the "Littler blue", as it is called, is a true Prussian blue with no trace of indigo or grey, and used in broad bands, to outline leaves, to colour alternate overlapping leaves, to fill reserves, or to paint flowers and views, its effect is decorative and gay in the extreme.

It must be remembered that gilding was used to relieve the washes of blue, but that as it was a size gilding of poor quality it is seldom that any trace of it now remains.* That its shortcomings were fully realised probably accounts for the use of an opaque white enamel which was painted over the blue in a manner much followed on contemporary salt-glazed ware. Diaper borders were not used at Longton Hall on blue and white porcelain, a fact which proves extremely useful in refuting the claims of many classes of porcelain which were once attributed to the factory! A border of slanting parallel blue dashes was, however, sometimes used, and is peculiar to Longton.

Transfer printing is very uncommon, so much so that there is considerable doubt whether any was ever undertaken. In addition to certain barrel-shaped mugs decorated in black transfer with Liverpool prints, there is also a class of ware decorated with floral borders in underglaze blue transfer, the remainder of the decoration being carried out in overglaze enamels (Plate 17). Exactly similar borders are to be found on undoubted Liverpool pieces (Plate 43) and it would appear that any printing found on Longton Hall porcelain was applied elsewhere, the articles being sent away for that purpose, or that at the sale of the factory undecorated ware was purchased and decorated by the buyers.

* See p. 175, note 11.

67

Chapter VIII

BRISTOL (REDCLIFF BACKS) BLUE AND WHITE PORCELAIN

IN THE year 1745 a company was formed consisting of Edward Heylyn of Bow, James Davis, and William Davis, to make porcelain in the Redcliff Backs Glasshouse at Bristol. The owner of the premises was William Lowdin, and for this reason the porcelain made thereat is often wrongly referred to as Lowdin's Bristol. Much controversy has arisen as the result of a contemporary letter written in 1750 by a Dr. Pococke, in which he writes that "I went to see a manufacture lately established here by one of the principals of the manufacture at Limehouse which failed. It is at a glasshouse". This statement has given rise to a speculation that a porcelain factory existed at Limehouse in addition to that at Bow, but there is no actual evidence to prove that this was indeed the case. It is much more likely that Heylyn of Bow, having been tempted to embark upon a porcelain-making enterprise at Bow, at the same time founded a works at Bristol, where, owing to its geographical position, he would be unlikely to experience the same difficulties of transport of raw materials which he must have encountered in London. The probable explanation of Dr. Pococke's statement is that the site of the Bow factory, on the north side of Stratford High Street, is very close indeed to Limehouse. Mr. Pountney, in his *Bristol Potteries*, has pointed out that Heylyn, who was with Thomas Frye, and who certainly took out a patent for a frit porcelain in 1744–5, was actually a Bristol man, well acquainted with the pottery trade. It would seem, therefore, that the Limehouse factory is a myth. In the 1750 letter already quoted, Dr. Pococke also says "lately established", and it has been argued that the origin of the factory was not very much previous to the year in which he wrote. There is, however, documentary evidence to prove that a lease of the kiln was bought by James Davis in 1745 from John Tandy, a brewer, who was the buyer of

Lowdin's lease. It is not likely that the process of actual manufacture would be long delayed. The factory had as short a life as had the original one at Bow. In 1751 the Worcester Porcelain Company was formed by Dr. John Wall and William Davis, the latter of whom took with him to Worcester two skilled workmen named Lyes and Podmore. At the same time Heylyn retired, and the factory closed down the following year, when all the business, together with moulds and patterns was transferred to Worcester, although unsold stock was retained and sold at the firm's warehouse in Castle Green, Bristol.

In contrast with the phosphatic or bone porcelain which was the characteristic product of the Bow factory, the porcelain made at Redcliff Backs was of steatite (or soapstone) composition, which produced a body common to the three great western factories of Worcester, Caughley, and Liverpool. This fact is quoted by Dr. Pococke in a letter dated October 1750, in which he refers to the "soapy rock" which was valued for making "porcelane" at Bristol.* It was very natural that these factories should choose to make use of steatite, since each was within easy reach of waterways at a time when water transport was the only cheap way of carrying heavy materials.

As with Bow, it is somewhat difficult to classify the productions of an experimental pioneer factory, but in the case of Redcliff Backs there is a certain amount of evidence. There exists a class of figures (with which we are not directly concerned) and of sauce or butter-boats, extremely few in number (the late Mr. Wallace Elliot, speaking before the English Porcelain Circle in 1928, had traced but six figures and eleven boats), which are marked with the word "Bristol" or "Bristoll" in relief. The sauce-boats are either white, blue painted, or enamelled. In addition to the marked specimens there is also a large quantity of exactly similar but unmarked pieces. It is difficult to escape the conclusion that the marked pieces were intended as samples, and were, therefore, the earliest productions of the factory, which, when approved by the trade, were produced on a commercial scale. The pieces so identified are of soft paste, which is very blued, as is the glaze, giving rise to a dark green colour by transmitted light, with lighter pin-holes here and there. In the thicker parts the body is opaque. The glaze is

* See p. 174, note 9.

extremely thin except in pools inside the foot rim, and has an uneven surface covered with little hollows rather like orange skin. The potting was inclined to be clumsy and the ware gives an impression of fumbling workmanship.

At a later period the porcelain produced was very similar to the early Worcester wares of which it was the forerunner, although not possessing the superior finish of the later factory. Thus we find the intense green hue and the thin glaze, which, however, was controlled beneath the foot, that is, it completely covered the foot. It is often disfigured by tiny black spots over the whole of the surface. These later productions were thinner and much more carefully potted than the earlier specimens.

The third class of ware associated with Redcliff Backs is known as the "scratch cross" family. Specimens of this ware bear incised marks, a cross or one or two short strokes, a cut on the foot rim, or both. All are steatitic. Similarly marked fragments were excavated on the site of the Bow factory, and there were thus some grounds for classifying the "family" as Bow. On chemical analysis, however, such specimens proved to be phosphatic. In summarising the rival claims of Bow and Redcliff Backs (or Bristol-Worcester, since there can be no sharp dividing line between the two factories), Mr. Wallace Elliot made the following points. In favour of a Bow origin there is the fact that the shape of the scratch cross mugs frequently found is identical with the Bow fragments, that the shape is characteristic of Bow, that the incised cross is found on Bow porcelain, and that if the marks indicate an experimental paste there would be no object in thus marking pieces made at a factory (Redcliff Backs) already using a steatitic paste. On the other side of the question he made reference to the chemical analysis already mentioned, the presence of an incised stroke on a sauce-boat marked "Bristoll", the presence of identical workmen's marks on scratch cross pieces and on pieces of both Worcester and Redcliff Backs, and a similarity of decoration on all three classes.

Since both factories, Redcliff Backs and Bow, were under the same management, I do not think that the question of the characteristic Bow shape is any evidence of Bow origin, since Heylyn would naturally use similar methods (apart from the difference in paste), shapes, and decoration in both the factories under his control. It has been suggested that scratch cross specimens are of Liverpool manufacture, but little convincing proof has been produced to support the claim which I think is fully refuted by the strong evidence just discussed. On the whole it would appear to be reasonable, in the absence of further information, to include the ware among the productions of the Bristol factory.

Now to consider the features which will help us to identify Redcliff Backs porcelain. Among the specimens classified by means of the Bristol or Bristoll mark are certain hexagonal butter-boats of small size. Such a one before me as I write (Plate 18) has a very rough base, thickly coated with a deep blue glaze which has left small portions of the paste (still blued, but creamy by contrast) uncovered. The sides rise to a wavy edge and are moulded in a silver shape. The handle is also moulded, is flat-sided, and has a thumb-rest at the top. By artificial light the blued body is an intense green with lighter pin-holes. On each side is a Chinese scene painted in a somewhat microscopic manner in a weak, blurred, greyish-blue, and flower-sprays are used to decorate the rest of the outside, regardless of the form of the moulding. Inside the rim on either side is painted a scallop shell, with others inside the lip and near the handle, while between them are four of the Chinese "eight precious objects", namely, the artemisia leaf, a jewel, a painting, and a scroll. In the bottom is a peony. The inside of the rim in many such specimens is painted with festoons of flowers, but the shell inside the lip is very characteristic. The sauce-boats belonging to this class are of unusually elongated shape, with S-shaped twists to the upper parts of their handles, the tops of which are flush with the rims. Among the mouldings we find a handle terminating in rosettes which spread snugly over the body, and reserves of leafy scrolls in relief. Pickle or sweetmeat-trays moulded in the shape of scallop shells were made in large quantities.

Finally, the Chinese landscapes often include palm-like plants and trees, water shaded in horizontal lines (although this device is common to many factories), a tree (?) shaped like the mast of a ship, complete with spars, and a pair of pyramids.

It has already been stated that the wares of the later period were

PLATE 18

REDCLIFF BACKS

a HEXAGONAL BUTTER-BOAT. Length, 4¼ in. Unmarked. About 1750–55.

b BOWL. Diameter, 5 in. Workman's mark. About 1750–55.

There are many variations of moulding in these hexagonal Redcliff Backs butter-boats, the prototypes of which were marked BRISTOL or BRISTOLL. Incidentally, similar pieces were made in the white at the Worcester factory after the moulds had been taken there. The flower-painting seen on the bowl is characteristic, and is executed in the same greyish, pale blue which was used on the butter-boat. The potting of the bowl is very like Worcester, but its paste is neither so pure (being disfigured by black specks) nor its glaze so clear as would be expected from that factory.

PLATE 18

a

b

73

similar to the early products of the Worcester factory. Indeed, it is quite impossible to differentiate between the two, and the term Bristol-Worcester is used to denote specimens of late Bristol and very early Worcester. Exceptions are the pieces already mentioned, in which the workmanship falls short of the high standard attained at Worcester during even the earliest years. On such specimens the glaze is spotted, and the decoration is usually rendered in the rather weak and lifeless blue previously described. It is noticeable, too, that owing to the running of the colour used in such decoration, the undecorated inside of a bowl or other article is often considerably whiter than the decorated exterior.

With the scratch cross family I have already dealt. Specimens are scarce, but are readily recognisable by the mark in conjunction with the Worcester type paste and decoration, and, frequently, with a workman's mark in blue. It will, however, be as well to ascertain whether any specimen so marked is really soft paste, since much hard paste Continental porcelain bears similar scratched or incised marks.

Chapter IX

WORCESTER BLUE AND WHITE PORCELAIN

It is usual to find that the average dealer's stock includes a dozen pieces of Worcester blue and white to every single specimen of any other make. Usually also the general dealer in antiques who has not made a special study of porcelain is apt to use the name "Wall Worcester" as a trade term, which he applies to any piece of blue and white. Such a state of affairs is natural enough, since, as we shall see, the Worcester factory was founded upon a sure financial basis, with men possessed of sound business ability, artistic discernment, and the necessary technical skill as its directors. With everything in their favour it is not surprising that their immediate success enabled them to develop a factory which was capable of supplying an enormous amount of fine porcelain (which was chiefly blue and white in the early days) to an eager public.

Many reasons have been given for the founding of a porcelain factory in Worcester, a city remote from any available source of raw materials. Political considerations and the desire to give employment in a city possessing few industrial opportunities may have had a certain amount of influence, but I imagine that the leading spirit of the venture, Dr. John Wall, was moved rather by a desire to further the development of the manufacture of the new and beautiful porcelain ware than by any political or industrial motives. He was a successful Worcester doctor, a capable chemist, an artist of ability, and, moreover, one who had been reared in surroundings redolent of art and of culture in the home of his guardian Mr. Samuel Sandys, afterwards Baron Sandys of Ombersley, Worcestershire. Whatever the motive may have been, Dr. Wall and fourteen other gentlemen, among them a painter, a goldsmith, a chemist, and several city business men, subscribed £4,500 in 1751 for the declared purpose of making porcelain, and a deed of partnership was drawn up. Dr. Wall was already possessed of the secret of

76

PLATE 19

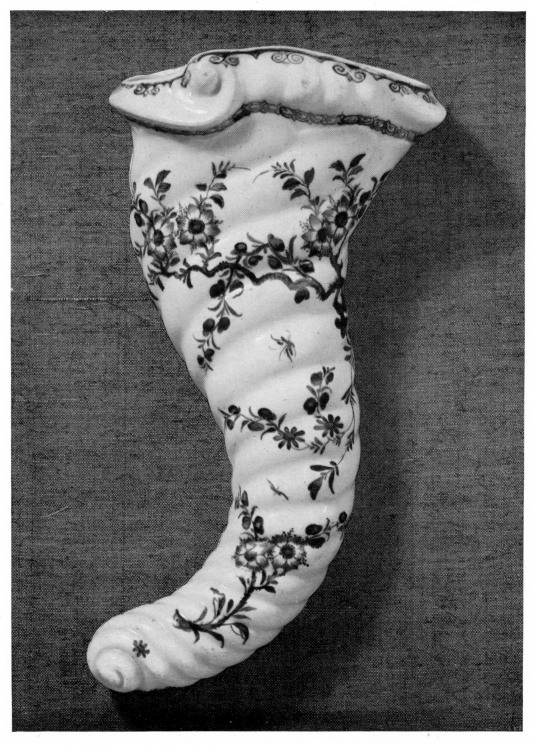

WORCESTER CORNUCOPIA. Length, 12 in. Crossed swords mark. About 1765.

The flower-holders moulded in this and other forms were made in pairs so as to hang symmetrically. As the mark denotes, the floral decoration, which is painted, is in the Meissen style.

porcelain manufacture, as has already been related. He had been in touch with William Davis, of Redcliff Backs fame, and had persuaded him to become one of the directors of the new factory, bringing with him, in addition to his share of the capital, two skilled workmen, Lyes and Podmore, and a quantity of moulds and finished ware. Thus was formed the "Worcester Tonquin Manufacture", with its headquarters in Warmstry House, an old mansion conveniently situated on the riverside.

The success of the factory can be traced from the frequent public advertisements of the sale of increasingly large amounts of ware, and by the establishment of a London warehouse in 1756, a success which continued until the sale of the establishment in 1783, Dr. Wall having died seven years before. With the sale came the end of what is always known as the Wall Period.

The new owner was the London agent of the company, Thomas Flight, who gave the business to his sons, Joseph and John. At the same time the chief decorator, Robert Chamberlain, left to found a factory of his own, and for some time produced porcelain in conjunction with Turner of Caughley in a manner which will be discussed later. The Flights, however, although they speedily introduced reforms which included the adoption of a new bone-ash paste to replace the old steatitic one, continued to produce blue and white in the old style in lessening quantities up to the end of the century. During this time John Flight died (in 1791) and Martin Barr took his place in 1793. The later history of the factory, relating the story of its ever-increasing success and of the splendid ware produced, is outside the scope of this book and may conveniently be studied elsewhere.

Early Worcester porcelain is an extremely beautiful and serviceable ware. It is hard looking and resists the file although it is of soft paste steatitic composition, which made it easily able to withstand boiling water. It did not stain. At its best it resembled very faithfully the Chinese porcelain which it was intended to imitate. In unglazed portions the paste is usually of a creamy hue, although the addition of cobalt sometimes gives a greyish tone. Cobalt was added also to the glaze, resulting in specimens of bluish tint. No rule can be laid down, however, since much blue and white appears to have had no cobalt

PLATE 20

WORCESTER

CORNUCOPIA. Length, 8½ in. Unmarked. About 1755.

Flower-holders in the form of cornucopia are among the most beautiful decorative pieces of Worcester or, indeed, of any porcelain. The moulding is well defined, and the painting exquisite. The specimen illustrated is one of a pair, its companion being symmetrically opposite in moulding and painting. Salt-glazed cornucopia were made in Staffordshire from a similar mould.

PLATE 20

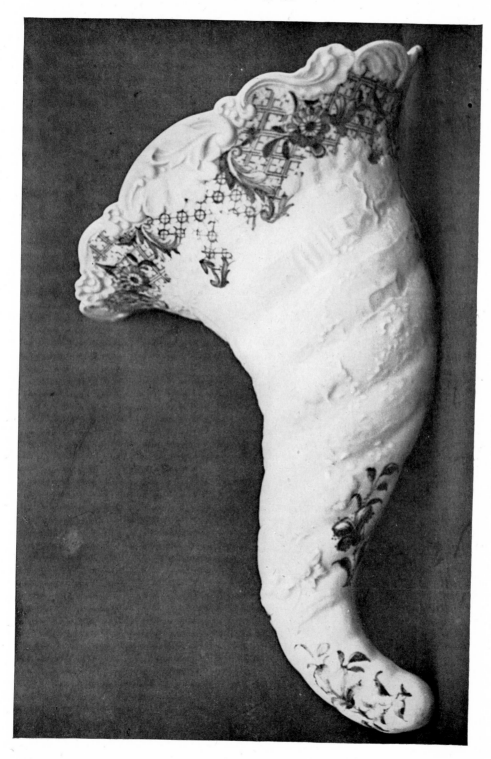

PLATE 21

PLATE 21

WORCESTER

DISH.   Diameter, 8 in.   Simulated Chinese mark.   About 1755.

Among the "Hundred Antiques" which form the decoration of this dish may be seen musical instruments reminiscent of the culture of the educated Chinese —these at least are recognisable by western eyes, but the remainder are symbolical and, therefore, meaningless to the unenlightened, although they form an extremely decorative pattern. Paste, glaze, and tone of blue are typical Worcester.

whatever added to it, and so remains quite creamy and, to modern eyes, all the more attractive. Thus it is that by artificial light, although much Worcester has the greenish hue which at one time was considered to be a sure test of authenticity, there is much that is pale yellow, approaching the straw colour more usually associated with Caughley. The lead glaze was close fitting and never crazed,* and it is rare to find any specimen in which it has collected in pools, either beneath the foot rim or elsewhere. As it was brushed on, it is a common feature to find uncovered biscuit patches inside the foot rim, but this is not peculiar to Worcester. So good was the potting that it was seldom necessary to grind the foot rims, as was so often the custom elsewhere. The Worcester paste was, as has been said, extremely good, but nevertheless there appears to have been some difficulty in making plates and dishes due to distortion in the kiln, whereas the material was excellent for making articles in the round. Mr. Hurlbutt has put forward this as a possible reason for the comparative scarcity of Worcester plates and saucers, even taking into consideration the fact that but one saucer was supplied with both a tea and a coffee-cup. It is certainly true that it is a wise custom to purchase an odd Worcester saucer on the certainty that sooner or later a cup will turn up to match it!

It seems almost certain that the frit porcelain made at Worcester was mainly blue and white, and that it consisted mostly of domestic ware. The more elaborate decorative articles were not as a rule attempted, although there are in existence several ambitious pieces which include an enormous tureen and cover elaborately moulded and decorated with Chinese scenes and flowers, $17\frac{1}{2}$ in. in length (Dyson Perrins Collection); a hexagonal flower-pot finely painted with flowering shrubs and birds, $12\frac{1}{2}$ in. high (Dyson Perrins Collection), and variously shaped vases decorated in different styles, among which the largest is a truly magnificent specimen in the same collection, made in several parts in the Chinese fashion, decorated all over with a perfectly drawn and elaborate Chinese landscape, and approximately three feet in height. Such pieces were the exception, but serve as sufficient proof that it was not due to any lack of technical ability that the more ordinary workaday wares were made, but rather that

* See p. 171, note 3.

shrewd business acumen decided rightly upon an appeal to the larger and more profitable demand for usable articles.

A large proportion of the early ware was moulded in silver shapes, because Samuel Bradley was a goldsmith and silversmith. To him also we can attribute the impeccable style of such pieces, which were always faultlessly moulded, never overdecorated, and never of unpleasing form. It is possible by a study of the collection of blue and white in the museum attached to the Royal Porcelain Works at Worcester to make a fairly comprehensive list of the patterns which were produced, which are as follows :—

Hexagonal cups and saucers decorated with Chinese scenes and made of the finest porcelain.

Cups and saucers moulded in several styles, which included a wavy or feather pattern (Plate 26), ribbed flutes, embossed floral scrolls, pine embossment, hollow flute, fine wavy ribs, waved leaf, fluted pattern lower half only, jointed ribs, petal pattern, and chrysanthemum petal pattern (Plate 26).

Cabbage leaf jugs, with or without mask lip (Plates 27 and 31).

Vine leaf dessert-dishes and pickle-dishes.

Salt-spoons, caddy-spoons, and gravy-spoons.

Knife and fork handles.

Embossed sauce-boats of all descriptions (Plate 24).

Double handled sauce-boats (Plate 23).

Embossed cream-jugs, and "sparrow-beak" cream-jugs.

Bell-shaped mugs and coffee-cups, the latter with moulded handles (Plates 22 and 23).

Tea-caddies (or tea-poys), ovoid, round, or square.

Eye-cups, hand candlesticks, and feeding-cups (Plate 33).

Oval and round butter-dishes with stands and covers, pierced and unpierced.

Baskets, pierced oval, round, and flanged round (Plate 2).

Small covered soup-tureens, with branch handles.

Embossed salad-bowls (Plate 34).

Cornucopia (Plates 19 and 20), strainers, egg-drainers (Plate 22), and vases.

Leaf-shaped comports and perforated comports.

PLATE 22

WORCESTER

a   EGG-DRAINER.   Length, 5 in.   Open crescent mark.   About 1755.

b   COFFEE-CUP.   Height, 2 in.   Workman's mark.   About 1755.

Nothing could be daintier than these small Worcester pieces. Both are thinly potted, the egg-drainer in particular being egg-shell in its seeming fragility. Unpierced specimens made in the same mould are also found, and are then intended for use as caddy-spoons. The small bell-shaped mugs were made with several varieties of handle.

PLATE 22

a

b

87

PLATE 23

a

b

c

PLATE 23

WORCESTER

a MUG. Height, 3½ in. Workman's mark. About 1755–60.

b MUG. Height, 4¼ in. Open crescent mark. About 1755–60.

c SAUCE-BOAT. Length, 7½ in. Workman's mark. About 1755.

Although similar in shape and in decoration, the mugs illustrated represent two classes of porcelain made at Worcester. The smaller is thinly potted, referred to by the factory as "fine porcelain", and now known as "egg shell", whereas the other is made of thick porcelain. The style of decoration, found in numerous varieties, is known as "root ornament", and is of Chinese origin. Two-handled sauce-boats are uncommon, and belong to the class of ware at one time considered to be Bow, owing to the wrong interpretation of the significance of the Chinese character for "jade", with which some of them are marked.

Pierced basket-work stands (resembling dishes).

Octagonal powder-blue plates (Plate 2).

Ornamental flower holders.

Plates moulded in various patterns and with variously shaped edges
(Plates 30 and 33).

It will be seen how great was the variety of mouldings used, usually
in conjunction with blue-painted flowers, Chinese landscapes, or
diaper borders. Particularly pleasing are those pieces which rely for
their effect upon moulding alone, with only a blue diaper border to
relieve the monotony of the white porcelain (Plate 25). Many of the
shapes figuring in the list are so characteristic of the factory that their
form alone is almost sufficient to identify them. It will be helpful,
therefore, to devote some time to their consideration. First, the moulding of the various tea and coffee services. As has already been noted,
there are at least ten of them, and of these there are hardly any that
appear on other porcelains, even on Caughley, where many Worcester
shapes were copied. Thus the collector will be on fairly safe ground
should he unhesitatingly classify pieces moulded in any of the given
patterns as being of Worcester origin without reference to any other
factory, always provided that he is satisfied that they were not made
at Redcliff Backs, where, as we have already seen, some of the Worcester
moulds originated. He will quickly find that his diagnosis will be upheld by paste, glaze, and decoration. A class of ware which has caused
much controversy consists of certain two-handled sauce-boats. They
have been ascribed to Bow, but as has already been mentioned in the
chapter dealing with that factory, it has now been finally agreed that
they are Worcester (Plate 23). I know of no similar two-handled pieces
being made elsewhere. The "sparrow beak" cream-jug was very popular at the Worcester factory and specimens are often found. So called
by reason of the peculiar pointed lip, Worcester examples are always
well covered by the decoration, and the loop handle, whether flat,
round, or grooved, is always of pleasing shape in contrast with the ugly
curves often assumed by the handles on similar jugs from other factories. Many of them are heavily potted and were evidently intended
for everyday use. Indeed, not only in jugs but also in practically every
article intended for domestic use, these two classes of porcelain, thickly

and thinly potted, are found, the latter often thin enough to merit the term "egg-shell" which is sometimes applied to them. Cylindrical mugs were made in large numbers and were decorated in countless ways. They invariably have grooved loop handles, their sides are parallel except that the rims sometimes bell out very slightly, and they have wide, well potted, and shallow foot rims (Plates 25 and 28). Small cups formed of overlapping leaves in silver style with a peculiar carefully moulded base in which the leaves radiate from a circle, are peculiar to the factory, as are the graceful wall vases moulded in the form of cornucopia (Plate 20). Covered butter-dishes with stands were made in several shapes, the most common being cylindrical, with twin moulded handles to accommodate which pieces are cut out of the cover, handles moulded to resemble twigs, and applied flowers at the terminals on both cover and stand. Sauce-boats were made in infinite variety and many patterns were copied by other factories, but the superior potting, absence of disfiguring blemishes, and clear, close-fitting glaze are usually deciding factors in arriving at correct diagnosis (Plate 24). Mention has already been made of the cabbage-leaf jugs with or without mask lips. These were made in various sizes and can be distinguished from the Lowestoft variety by reason of their better shape, since the Lowestoft jugs are usually lopsided or otherwise mis-shapen, and from those made at Caughley by their decoration. Worcester made more varieties of spoon (not only tea-spoons) than any other factory; indeed, with the exception of an egg-shaped caddy-spoon made at Bow after a Chinese model, I know of no other factory which made these dainty articles. Especially beautiful are the caddy-spoons which have a moulded flower at the end of the handle; they are so light and cleanly potted. When pierced, these spoons were in-tended for use as egg-drainers (Plate 22)—a long-felt want even in modern homes, and maybe in those days a capital advertisement of the much vaunted boiling-water-resisting claim! Bell-shaped mugs were produced in two varieties, both with grooved loop handles, but whereas one style has the usual type of foot rim common to tea and coffee-cups, the other, which is usually of the thicker type of porcelain, stands on a thick rounded base (Plate 23). Tea-caddies were made in three styles—box shape, ovoid, and round. Many have the usual

PLATE 24

WORCESTER

d is a CREAM-JUG, the others are SAUCE-BOATS. Lengths, from 6 in. (*d*) to 7 in. (*b* and *e*). Marks: *b* and *d* have workmen's marks, *c*, *e*, and *f* have open crescents. About 1755–60.

The beautiful moulding of these sauce-boats is typical of Worcester practice. All were made in different sizes, with differing decoration, although usually Chinese in origin. An example of this is shown by a comparison of "*b*" and "*e*". It is interesting to note that the placing of the decoration is not always in keeping with the lines of the moulding. As with so much blue and white Worcester, many fine sauce-boats are unmarked.

PLATE 24

a c b

d e f

PLATE 25

a   b   c

d   e   f

PLATE 25

WORCESTER

a COFFEE-CUP. Height, 2¼ in. Chinese symbol mark. About 1755.

b MUG. Height, 5½ in. Open crescent mark. About 1755.

c CREAM-JUG. Height, 2¾ in. Open crescent mark. About 1755.

d COFFEE-POT. Height, 8 in. Open crescent mark. About 1755–60.

e COFFEE-POT. Height, 8½ in. Open crescent mark. About 1755.

f COFFEE-POT. Height, 5½ in. Unmarked. About 1770.

N.B. *f* is transfer printed

"Long Eliza" decoration is seen in many different forms on all makes of porcelain. The coffee-cup is an exact copy of a Chinese piece, and bears an uncommon mark, since, although the Chinese character "jade" is frequently found in the form of a workman's mark, it is rarely seen drawn so large as on this specimen, filling the entire base. The border inside the rim is also of Chinese origin, of a type known as "triangular work". The large mug is typical of those made at Worcester, with its greater diameter near the foot. The decoration which it bears is commonly found on mugs, cups, and jugs. Barrel-shaped cream-jugs were made both at Worcester and at Caughley, decorated in similar manner.

Dragon patterns copied from the Chinese were used at Bow, Worcester, and Caughley. The example pictured is an exact copy of a Chinese piece in my possession: it is a most pleasing form of decoration, especially when it is so used (as on cups, saucers, bowls, etc.) that the dragon covers both outside and inside of the article. In order to distinguish it from the Caughley version, which is usually printed and known as the "Broseley Dragon", this variety is known as the "Worcester Dragon". The effective use of moulded decoration, either in conjunction with blue-painted borders or left entirely in the white, attained a high standard at Worcester. The coffee-pot illustrated is moulded in the "chrysanthemum" pattern. The transfer printed pot is made in the thicker porcelain used for everyday wares, and is decorated with a pattern commonly used both at Worcester and at Caughley. Indeed, engraved copper plates are in existence which are known to have been made by Thomas Turner, and which bear his initials.

PLATE 26

WORCESTER

TEA-BOWLS, COFFEE-CUPS, AND SAUCERS. Diameters (saucers):
From 4¾ in. (*b*) to 4½ in. (*d*). Marks: *b* and *c* have open crescents,
a and *f* have workmen's marks, *d* and *e* have the script capital W. About
1755–65.

Cups and saucers decorated in various styles. From left to right the moulded
patterns were described by the proprietors as "fluted", "feather", and
"chrysanthemum" patterns. The "root ornament" on the fluted specimens
should be compared with that on specimen "*d*"; there are many varieties of
this effective Chinese decoration.

PLATE 26

a   b   c

d   e   f

PLATE 27

a

b

PLATE 27

WORCESTER

a BOWL. Diameter, 8 in. Open crescent mark. About 1760.

b JUG. Height, 8 in. Crossed swords and script "*e*" mark. About 1760.

The bowl is painted with a Chinese scene by an artist whose work is characterised by the freedom and sureness of his brushwork. The jug is an example of
the Worcester "cabbage leaf" moulding, but without the usual mask lip.
Similar jugs were made at Lowestoft, but they are usually misshapen. The
flower-painting is carried out in an extremely pure sapphire blue, a very good
imitation of the Oriental pigment. As would be expected from the Meissen
mark, the decoration is in Meissen style. Incidentally, the mark itself is unusual
in that it is usual to find a 9 or 91 between the blades of the swords, whereas
the symbol used in this example is neither, and is between the handles.

Worcester open-flower knob. Certain small, dainty bell-shaped coffee-cups with moulded handles were peculiar to the factory (Plate 22). Last, but by no means least, are the singularly beautiful pierced baskets, fashioned to resemble trellis or wicker-work. There are many varieties, but a feature of them all is the fact that moulded flowers were applied beneath the intersections of the wicker-work. Some are handled with tiny twig handles, and they may be either oval, round (Plate 2), or with flanged edges. Stands and covers supplied with them are likewise pierced.

So far no mention has been made of the styles of painting and printing to be found on Worcester blue and white. Of the pigment itself little can be said, insomuch as, in common with other factories, there was great variation of colour between a pure sapphire blue vieing with the Oriental in clarity, and a dark indigo which becomes more pronounced during later years. Mention of the powder-blue plates also made at Bow, Caughley, and Lowestoft has been made on previous pages, and the point must again be stressed that the superior potting of the Worcester variety, especially in regard to the foot rim, is sufficient guide to their origin. The flower painting was almost exclusively in the Oriental style, but a notable exception was the use of the vine leaf and tendrils as a motif. Mention may be made again of subjects copied from the Chinese, among which are found the much sought "Eloping Bride", "St. George and the Dragon", the "Hundred Antiques", "Long Elizas" in various forms, an owl and other birds in a tree, and Chinese landscapes of every description (Plate 27). Perhaps the most beautiful of all is a pattern of Chinese subjects in leaf-shaped reserves on a marbled blue ground sprinkled with hawthorn blossoms, which is found on cylindrical mugs of various sizes (Plate 28). Among later styles of decoration an outstanding pattern is that known as the "Blue Lily" (Plate 35). This is again of Chinese derivation, and was chosen in 1788 by George III and his Queen when on a visit to the factory. The pattern was then renamed the "Queen Charlotte" or "Royal Lily" design. It consists of radial panels of conventional lilies, and was usually enriched with gilding, a practice which, incidentally, was most uncommon in the early life of the factory,* at which time the absence of any sort of gilding on blue and

* See p. 175, note 11.

white ware was a further tribute to the artistic sense of the management.

As far as can be ascertained transfer printing was introduced at Worcester in 1756, the method having been brought by Robert Hancock * from Battersea, where he had been employed as a printer on enamels. It is irrelevant to enter into the controversy as to whether Liverpool or Worcester first printed on porcelain, suffice it to say that the process having first proved to be successful in overglaze enamels, in black, lilac, and red, it was probably adapted to decoration in underglaze blue in 1756. Evidence in support of this date has been discussed in an earlier chapter, and it is, of course, obviously probable that blue printing would be begun hard upon the heels of the overglaze method, so urgent was the demand for blue and white. At one time it was supposed that blue printing began as late as 1770, in which year the blue painters, doubtless in fear lest their services should be in less demand as a result of the success of the printing process, came out on strike. But even without any other evidence the style of many of the prints makes such a late date most improbable, even if we could believe that the management could have been so unbusinesslike as to neglect such an obvious opportunity!

Worcester blue transfer ware is far superior to any other in neatness of execution and fittingness for its purpose, because the size and shape of the pattern is always calculated properly and adequately to cover the article without the fault of over-decoration. Doubtless Robert Hancock himself would be responsible for the production of many of the designs, and there is evidence to show that he imparted his skill to a "school" of engravers, among whom were included Thomas Turner (later to do much fine work at Caughley), Valentine Green (who became engraver to George III), and James Ross.

The subjects from which the engravers drew their inspiration have already been dealt with, and there is no need to dwell on them further. As in the case of the printed patterns, there are nevertheless certain subjects which were extremely popular on Worcester porcelain. The most famous of them all, a group of conventionalised fruit and flowers which includes an object resembling a fir cone or a strawberry, was

* See p. 176, note 13.

PLATE 28

WORCESTER

MUG. Height, 5 in. Open crescent mark. About 1760–65.

It is difficult to imagine a more beautiful style of decoration than this. The blue is "marbled", and provides a most pleasing contrast to the white blossoms scattered upon it. In the original Chinese form the blue ground, netted with darker lines, was intended to represent the cracking ice which symbolised the ending of winter and the coming of the New Year, which was further emphasised by the early-flowering plum blossom reserved in white upon it. Such Worcester mugs were made in several sizes, and the smaller ones such as this are rare.

PLATE 28

PLATE 29

a

b

PLATE 29

WORCESTER

a BOWL. Diameter, 7½ in. Open crescent mark. About 1760–70.

b SUCRIER AND COVER. Diameter (sucrier), 3½ in. Open crescent mark. About 1770.

An example of reticent, well-balanced decoration, and of a typical Worcester shape. The border should be compared with the Bow version in Plate 9. It has been pointed out in the text that Worcester blue and white porcelain is invariably well covered by its decoration, but never overdecorated. This feature is well exemplified in this covered sucrier. Notice the "pineapple" border, which is painted on the outside of the cover and on the inside of the sucrier.

PLATE 30

WORCESTER

a CRESS-DISH. Diameter, 7½ in. Open crescent mark. About 1765.

b PLATE. Diameter, 9¾ in. Hatched crescent mark. About 1770. Transfer printed.

Cress-dishes are uncommon—they are intended, of course, to stand upon large bowls. This particular example has a border pattern which is commonly found painted on printed wares (see Plate 33). The plate has "basket-work" moulding, and is printed with a sprig pattern which is common in both printed and painted form on both Worcester and Caughley wares. It is known as the "Chantilly sprig", after the Continental factory whence it originated (see Plate 41).

PLATE 30

a

b

PLATE 31

a

b

PLATE 31

WORCESTER (Transfer printed wares)

a SPITTOON. Height, 4½ in. Hatched crescent mark. About 1775.

b JUG. Height, 12 in. Hatched crescent mark. About 1775.

Specimens of this shape are often dignified by the name of "vase", whereas in fact they were intended for use as spittoons! Nevertheless, they are of pleasing form. The mask jug is a typical example of one of the largest sizes. Although so large, and of necessity thickly potted, the quality of the paste is such that the typical Worcester green reaction to transmitted light is clearly visible in every part.

PLATE 32

WORCESTER

TEA-BOWL AND SAUCER.   Saucer diameter, 4½ in.   About 1770.   Mark,
hatched crescent.   Blue transfer printed.

The "Two Milkmaids" is one of Hancock's happiest efforts, and is very rare
in underglaze blue, though common enough in enamel. The darker patches of
colour which can be seen in the border are actually blobs of red, which rather
spoil the delicate effect of the blue printing. Similar pieces were made at
Caughley.

PLATE 32

PLATE 33

a   *b*

c

112

PLATE 34

WORCESTER (Transfer printed wares)

a SALAD-BOWL. Diameter, 11 in. Hatched crescent mark. About 1770–75.

b, c and *d* COFFEE-CUPS AND SAUCERS. Various diameters (saucers). Hatched crescent marks. About 1770–75.

Bowls such as this were intended for use as salad bowls, but are sometimes referred to as junket bowls. The central print is the well-known "strawberry" or "pine cone" pattern, but the smaller ones are examples of the English style of printing. The outside of the bowl is decorated with prints of vegetables. The cups and saucers are cleanly printed, two with adaptations of Chinese land-scapes, the other with a Meissen design.

PLATE 34

a

b   *c*   *d*

PLATE 35

PLATE 35

WORCESTER   (Flight Period)

TEA-POT.   Height, 6 in.   Mark: Incised B.   About 1790.

This tea-pot of the Flight period is decorated with the "Royal Lily" or "Queen Charlotte" pattern.

copied at Caughley, Lowestoft, and Liverpool (Plate 33). Prints of vegetables were entirely peculiar to the factory, and are particularly fitting when used on both the inside and outside of certain large moulded salad-bowls (Plate 34). A popular Chinese landscape features a zigzag fence with a large spray of flowers above it, an island, and a pair of flying birds (Plate 34); and yet another has a fence surmounted by palm-shaped trees, and an island on which is a signpost-like erection (Plate 34). After a Meissen original is a spray of flowers which included a single large rose, together with several small sprays and a butterfly (Plate 34). From the French was copied a design featuring a large cornflower or carnation around which are smaller prints of flowers and a butterfly. This very common pattern, which was also used at Caughley, was known as the Chantilly decoration (Plate 30). Several of Hancock's designs, originally intended and used for overglaze printing, were utilised for printing in blue, among them the "two milkmaids", "parrot and grapes" (Plate 38), and "ruined temple". In common with the painted wares great use was made of diaper borders in Chinese style, which were simple in conception, and never ornate or complicated as at Caughley or Liverpool. Alternatively, single or double lines were often used, as was a circle of blue in the bottoms of cups and bowls. In many cases both painted and printed decoration were used on the same piece (Plate 33).

Blue and white wares in the early styles continued in scarcely unabated popularity until the end of the Wall period, and there are many dated examples of late date, including, for instance, a mug painted with St. George and the Dragon, and dated 1776, in the Dyson Perrins Collection. There is also a class of pieces printed in a somewhat brighter violet-toned blue, which by reason of their paste and typical Worcester potting do not seem to be of Salopian origin. That they are late seems to be indicated by the poor quality of the printing, which would seem to have been done from much worn plates, so much so that it is sometimes difficult to decide whether the decoration is painted or printed. Such pieces probably date from the beginning of the Flight period.

Chapter X

CAUGHLEY BLUE AND WHITE PORCELAIN

I⊤ is probable that the greater part of the blue and white porcelain exhibited in the dealers' shops originated at the neighbouring factories of Worcester and Caughley. There is, however, this difference between the two, that whereas the former produced a large amount of polychrome ware almost from the very beginning, the latter confined itself to the production of blue and white to a greater extent than any other factory, almost, indeed, to the exclusion of enamelled goods. Strangely enough, despite this fact, Salopian blue and white porcelain (to give it its more usual name) has been much neglected, both by collectors and by writers on porcelain, despite the fact that its best products are fine enough to be easily mistaken for Worcester porcelain, which is the acme of perfection in both manufacture and decoration.

There remains to-day no trace of the Caughley factory, which was situated on the bank of the Severn near the town of Broseley, itself long famous for the manufacture of earthenware. A Mr. Gallimore established a pottery at Caughley in the year 1754, near to Caughley Hall, the residence of Ralph Brown, a relation, and owner of a pottery at the neighbouring village of Jackfield. Since Gallimore was a friend of the father of Thomas Turner, a pupil of Hancock of Worcester and himself an artist and engraver of note, it is possible that he may have had the help of workmen from Worcester, although it is doubtful whether porcelain was manufactured at Caughley during its earliest years. Certain it is, however, that when in 1772 Thomas Turner married Gallimore's daughter and came to Caughley, the manufacture of porcelain was undertaken and continued without a break until the closing of the factory in 1799. The old premises were enlarged and almost completely rebuilt by the year 1775, and it seems that Turner, who was a keen business man of abnormal energy and initiative, quickly saw that it was in his power to rival the Worcester factory in

PLATE 36

CAUGHLEY (Transfer printed)

TEA BOWL, COFFEE-CUP, SAUCERS, AND CREAM-JUGS.

a, *b*, *e*, and *g* have hatched crescent marks, *c* has disguised numerals. About 1775.

Three patterns commonly found on Caughley printed wares are illustrated here. That on the right is the "fisherman" pattern, engraved by Thomas Turner, and marked with two of the "disguised numerals" which were at one time thought to be Worcester marks. The central pattern is known as the "pheasant", and is found in several varieties, while that on the left is an adaptation of a Chinese garden scene.

Among the sparrow-beak jugs, *e* is of interest, as it is decorated in a style peculiar to the factory with an English landscape. Such prints are usually executed in the violet-toned blue which was invented by Turner. There are several variations.

PLATE 36

a   b   c

d   e   f   g

PLATE 37

PLATE 37

CAUGHLEY

MUG.   Height, $3\frac{1}{4}$ in.   Dated 22nd May, 1787.

This mug is fully discussed in the text (see p. 133). The different tones of blue used for the landscapes are indistinguishable in the photograph.

the production of the blue and white porcelain so much in demand. Not content, however, with the knowledge he had already gained at Worcester, in 1780 he toured the Continental factories, returning with several skilled workmen, new patterns of French origin, and the secret of a new violet-blue of strength and brilliance. Production continued on a large scale until 1799, when the factory was purchased by John Rose, a former apprentice at the factory, who had already opened a rival concern at Coalport on the opposite bank of the river. Finally, after some years of survival as a manufactory of biscuit porcelain, the Caughley premises were closed in 1814.

It has long been common knowledge that porcelain from Caughley, in the white, and also decorated in underglaze blue, was purchased by Chamberlain and Grainger at their Worcester factories in the early nineteenth century. In addition, however, it was held by Jewitt, as far back as 1885, that much of the printing on Worcester porcelain was done at Caughley. Apart from the fact already quoted that Turner was an engraver of talent, there was little actual proof to uphold Jewitt's statement.

However, there are certain pieces of undoubted Worcester potting bearing transfer decoration of the type attributed to Turner, some of which may, of course, have been done by him at Worcester, but others (including a large mug in the Dyson Perrins Collection, of which mention will be made later) which may very easily have been finished at Caughley. The blue in such cases is often of the Salopian violet tint.

In refuting Jewitt's suggestion, it has been pointed out that Turner's secession from Worcester may have been a likely cause of hostility between the factories. That this was not so is shown, in the first place, by the fact that truly enormous business was done with Chamberlain after Turner had gone to Caughley, as is clearly shown in the Chamberlain account books in the possession of Mr. Dyson Perrins; and in the second by the large amount of ware in existence which is clearly of Wall period paste, but which, on the evidence of the mark, was printed at Caughley. Broadly speaking, the classes of porcelain which owe some part of their finished state to both places of manufacture would appear to be as follows :—

1. Caughley porcelain decorated by Chamberlain and sold as

Worcester. Such pieces would be of the improved Turner paste, evolved in all probability after his visit in 1780 to France, and bought by Chamberlain until he was able to produce his own white ware.

2. Caughley porcelain decorated by Chamberlain and returned to Caughley. Thus we read in an account book of 1789 the following:—

> Feb. 6th 1789.
> To Thos. Turner Esq.
> For painting a "red border" on 11 pieces   3/10
> For gilding the same   4/3

(Classes 1 and 2 were probably the results of the period when Turner had gone to Caughley to teach them how to produce good porcelain, in which they were soon successful, whereas the Chamberlains were painters, not potters.)

3. Decorated Caughley porcelain bought by Chamberlain and sold either as received or with added decoration. Evidence of this type of ware is provided in another account book of the same year, in which we may read this extract:—

> Jan. 1789.
> Goods recd. from Thos. Turner Esq.
> 6 $\frac{1}{2}$ pint mugs—mulberry, at 1/–   6/–
> 6 ,,   ,,   parrot, at 1/–   6/–
> 12 ,,   ,,   flowers, at 1/–   12/–
> 12 ,,   ,,   fishing, at 1/–   12/–

and so on.

4. Porcelain made and printed in blue at Caughley and finished at the Flight factory. This is an exceedingly rare class, of which un-doubted examples are few. Mr. Dyson Perrins, however, has a large cider-mug printed all over with a brocade pattern in underglaze blue, with reserves in which are views painted in overglaze brown, with gilding. There are two marks, a Caughley concealed numeral 5 in underglaze blue, and an overglaze mark in brown which consists of the words "WORCESTER MANUFACTORY FLIGHT" in an oval, surmounted by a crown.

5. Soft white porcelain, similar to Turner's paste, but marked with a large blue crescent and FLIGHT'S impressed. Such pieces are

PLATE 38

CAUGHLEY

JUG.   Height, 6 in.   Unmarked.   About 1775.

A Caughley version of the cabbage-leaf jugs which were also made at Worcester, decorated with the "parrot and vine" print. A broad band of diaper is frequently found around the rim, and the blue is usually of the violet tone favoured by Turner.

PLATE 38

PLATE 39

PLATE 39

CAUGHLEY

DESSERT-DISH.   Length, 10 in.   Mark: filled-in capital C.   About 1775.

This fine dish formed part of a dessert service. It is an example of the dark, vigorous powder-blue sometimes used at Caughley, and the decoration is in Chinese style.

PLATE 40

CAUGHLEY

(Transfer printed wares)

a BUTTER-DISH, COVER AND STAND. Length (stand), 7½ in. Hatched crescent mark. About 1775.

b BUTTER-DISH, COVER AND STAND. Diameter (stand), 6½ in. Marks: C (dish), filled-in crescent (stand). About 1775.

Butter-dishes in these shapes were made at Worcester and at Caughley. The Chantilly pattern on the oval dish and cover is printed, but another specimen in my possession has the same decoration in painted form, identical in every other respect. Very fine moulded and pierced pieces were made at Caughley, but they are rare. Note the open flower-knob to the cover of the round dish.

PLATE 40

a

b

usually transfer printed, in underglaze blue of violet hue, and with subjects better known on porcelain of the Wall period. Close scrutiny will often show traces of wear in the engraved plate.

6. Worcester porcelain of the Wall period printed at Caughley. Many pieces belonging to this class are to be found, in which the paste is unmistakably Worcester, showing green by transmitted light, and the potting neat, with typical Worcester foot rim, but with one of the accepted Caughley marks. I have in my collection a pair of large moulded salad-bowls (Plate 34), identical in paste, which is definitely Worcester, and with printed decoration. The one has a hatched crescent mark, the other a capital C, a Caughley factory mark never used at Worcester. Possible alternatives are either that both were printed at Caughley, or that one was printed at Worcester and the other at Caughley, using engraved plates supplied by Worcester. However that may be, they were both certainly potted at the latter factory.

7. Worcester porcelain, either Chamberlain's or Flight's, printed at Caughley. A large mug in the Dyson Perrins Collection would seem to belong to this class. It was undoubtedly potted at Worcester, and judging by its paste it is fairly late, certainly too late to be of the Wall period. It is decorated with the well-known "parrot and vine" in underglaze blue, and also in underglaze blue is the capital S factory mark of Caughley. The only possible conclusion is that the Caughley mark was given to a prefabricated (Worcester) piece when the decoration was done at Caughley.

I have in my own collection a mug of Salopian porcelain which is probably unique. It is decorated in underglaze blue with eight practically identical Chinese scenes, separated by brush strokes, each scene painted in a slightly different tone of blue, and each bearing a letter of identification together with the word "Cobalt" (Plate 37). This mug would seem to belong to one or other of these classes, and the tone of the blues, together with the evidence of the Salopian potting, would seem to support the view that it was painted there in order that it might be sent to Chamberlain as a pattern. On the other hand, it might well be an early essay at decoration by Chamberlain of the untried white ware of Turner's introduction from the Salopian factory, since doubtless long experiment was necessary ere adequate knowledge was obtained of the "foreign" paste to enable decorators and workmen to secure the desired results.

It is doubtful whether any collector of Worcester porcelain has ever been able honestly to declare that his collection contains no single specimen of Caughley manufacture. I am in complete disagreement with those who contend that Worcester productions can always be distinguished by reason of their superior potting. Turner had undergone a long and careful apprenticeship at Worcester, he was fully versed in all the secrets of his craft, and his character and ability were such that, like Wedgwood, he would be unlikely to pass anything but the best. Much Caughley porcelain is fully equal to Worcester in potting, finish, and decoration, and we must rather look to quality of paste and glaze in order to differentiate between the two porcelains.

Caughley porcelain is usually of a creamier hue than Worcester, having a lesser degree of blueing of the paste. The glaze, although often thickly applied, has a dry appearance, as though some quality of the paste, of soapstone composition, has absorbed it. Small pools of the glaze are sometimes found on the bottoms of articles, an uncommon feature of Worcester porcelain. By transmitted light, as has been already said, the Caughley paste is of a cloudy orange or dark straw colour, in contrast with the greenish or bluish Worcester hue. Whereas the Worcester foot rim is usually triangular in section, that used at Caughley was more usually rectangular. The appearance of an incised ring on the bottoms of cups, saucers, etc., has often been claimed as a Caughley peculiarity, but such a mark is to be found on many other porcelains, and is merely a mark made by the turner while the article was being trimmed in the lathe. Most of the Caughley shapes and forms of decoration, painted and printed, were identical with those used at Worcester, with the exception of certain patterns, which will be described later, the early silver moulded wares so popular at Worcester. Yet another important fact is that the intense violet-blue introduced by Turner in his later wares is never found on porcelain painted or printed at Worcester.

By far the greater part of the Caughley production was composed of printed wares, and naturally so, since Turner was a skilled designer and engraver. In addition, it must be remembered that Robert Hancock left Worcester in 1775 in order to join Turner at Caughley, bringing with him not only his skill but his designs, and probably many plates engraved by him. On the whole, except in the Caughley-Hancock pieces, Caughley printing differs in several respects from that found on Worcester ware. The designs are masterpieces of draughtsmanship, and give the general impression that they were drawn with ruler and square to mathematical exactitude. Especially is this the case with Turner's Chinese subjects, in which the horizontal shading of the waves with perfectly parallel and widely spaced lines and the perfect clarity of line are characteristic. The same thing may be seen in floral subjects, in which the petals are shaded with the same parallel lines. Many of the patterns which are to be found on both Worcester and Caughley differ in that a broad diaper border is added to the outside, inside, or both of the rims of pieces from the latter factory, especially in the case of mugs and mask jugs. Gilding was used at Caughley to enrich diaper borders, but so far as I am aware it was never so used at Worcester. In fairness to Caughley, however, we must remember that the gilding may have been added by an outside decorator. A border much favoured was an exceptionally deep one composed of several elements of Chinese diaper in conjunction with butterflies, flowers, etc. Similar borders were used at Liverpool, but were not so well designed or executed. The rims of mugs, cream-jugs, sauce-boats, etc., were often decorated with a hazy blue line on the extreme edge (Plate 41).

Hancock's work is to be seen on Caughley porcelain in the shape of the "milkmaid" pattern after Gainsborough, a scene in classical style known as the "Panini ruins", and a design of a parrot eating grapes (Plate 38), all of which are to be found on Worcester porcelain, both in underglaze and overglaze printing. Turner himself will be remembered by his famous "Willow Pattern", introduced by him about 1780 as an adaptation of typical Chinese landscapes and afterwards used with interesting modifications by the whole pottery trade. His "Broseley Dragon" pattern, derived from the Chinese dragon, is more uncommon, and should not be confused with the somewhat similar beasts which were popular on Bow and Worcester porcelain in blue painting.

PLATE 41

CAUGHLEY

a   MUG.   Height, 3½ in.   Unmarked.   1778.

b   MUG.   Height, 6 in.   Hatched crescent mark.   About 1775–80.   Transfer printed.

Many presentation mugs were made at Caughley, of which this is an example. The "Chantilly sprig" here appears in painted form, and should be compared with the printed version on the other mug. Both have the blue line around the rim which is a feature of the factory.

PLATE 41

a

b

Vying with these patterns in popularity was the "Fisherman" pattern, which included a fishing-boat, a fisherman holding a fish, a duck with outspread wings, and a fisherman seated on the bank (Plates 5 and 36). This again was a copy from the Chinese.

Specimens bearing painted decoration, as I have implied, are not often found, and have no special characteristics apart from the occasional use of the violet blue, being similar to the Worcester products. Notable exceptions, however, are painted in underglaze powder-blue. Of these, one belongs to the class common to Bow, Worcester, and Lowestoft, with round and fan-shaped panels painted with Chinese scenes. The powder-blue is extremely pale and lifeless, with a coarse grain, and the drawing of the scenes has the trait of extreme accuracy already mentioned in references to the printing. The origin of these specimens is fully proved by the fact that some of them bear an impressed SALOPIAN in addition to a simulated Chinese mark (Plate 12). The other pattern has alternate panels of powder-blue, diaper, and Chinese emblems radiating from a central design of flowers rising from rocks, also in Chinese style (Plate 39). The powder-blue of these pieces, however, is much darker and stronger.

Chapter XI

LIVERPOOL BLUE AND WHITE PORCELAIN

The term "Liverpool" has been for a long time misused to describe any porcelain which defied certain identification. Very little is known of the many factories which flourished in that city during the latter part of the eighteenth century, engaged in the manufacture of earthenware or porcelain, or both, and less still of their productions. As a result, the uncertainty as to the sorts of ware made at any of them resulted in a lumping together of all the puzzle pieces under the one name, with little fear of contradiction. So it is that for some time, as knowledge has accumulated, many of these specimens have been relegated to their proper cabinets as Lowestoft, Longton Hall, or Bow. At the same time, however, a large amount of true Liverpool has been correctly identified, and the collections in the various museums contrive to display an extremely mixed range of wares which will be justified when it is realised how numerous were the factories engaged in the manufacture of porcelain in the city. Much of it is of inferior quality compared with other factories, and for this reason alone it has not received the attention which it deserves. In fact, much Liverpool porcelain is of the highest quality, and with this realisation it has acquired greater interest and, consequently, deeper study, with the result that, although even now imperfectly understood owing to lack of reliable evidence, it can be given a high place in the ranks of the early factories. In addition it can be classified with a fair degree of accuracy —the difficulty being not to decide whether a specimen was made in Liverpool, but to assign it to any particular factory. In the first place, then, what is known of these factories?

Much historical evidence is given in a book named *The History of the Art of Pottery in Liverpool*, written by Joseph Mayer and published in 1855. The writer mentions two factories, both of them advertised in *Williamson's Liverpool Advertiser and Mercantile Register*. Thus, in November 1756, attention is drawn to a "Liverpool China Manufactory" whose proprietors were Messrs. Reid and Co., and who sold "all kinds of blue and white china, not inferior to any make in England". This "china" may not have been porcelain, though it was stated by Jewitt in his *Ceramic Art of Great Britain* that porcelain was in fact made by the firm. Further references are made to this factory in the same newspaper up to the year 1761. Later in the year 1756, a firm by the name of Chaffers and Co. draws attention to a ware "sold nowhere in the town but at their manufactory on Shaw's Brow". It is known that Richard Chaffers was a potter by trade, who had been employed at Worcester in 1751, and who had arrived in Liverpool after a sojourn at Wedgwood's factory. After the death of Chaffers the factory was taken over by Philip Christian, who became the city's leading potter.

Other evidence is available to show that other potteries existed. When Sadler made his trials of transfer printing on porcelain in 1756 it is on record that among those present was a potter named Samuel Gilbody, and there is a mug in the Mayer Museum in Liverpool bearing his name as maker. The sale of Gilbody's factory was announced in the Press in July 1761.

Famous among Liverpool potters were the Pennington brothers, James, John, and Seth. The last, according to Jewitt, appears to have made porcelain. Sadler, also, in his notebook of 1769, gives a recipe for Seth Pennington's china, which, he says, contained bone-ashes and fritt. His factory, according to *Billinge's Liverpool Advertiser*, was sold in 1799.

Zachariah Barnes is mentioned by Mayer as a potter, a maker of tiles, char-pots, etc. He is mentioned as having given up the manufacture of porcelain and to have made delft.

Reference to lesser potters is made in the *London Gazette* of June 17th, 1800, which announces the dissolving of a partnership between Thomas Woolfe, Miles Mason, and John Lucock, trading as Thomas Woolf and Co., and in the *Liverpool Directory* of 1766 William Ball, Richard Chaffers, and Philip Christian are listed as prominent makers of "china".

Truly a formidable list. Assuming that the manufacture of porcelain was attempted by the majority of those whose names we have

14*   141

PLATE 42

LIVERPOOL (Zachariah Barnes)

a PICKLE-SHELL. Length, 5½ in. Unmarked. About 1770.

b POUNCE OR PEPPER-POT. Height, 3¼ in. Unmarked. About 1770.

c MUG. Height, 4½ in. Unmarked. About 1770.

All transfer printed

These specimens are typical of Zachariah Barnes's porcelain. The pounce-pot (used to sprinkle sand on wet writing before the invention of blotting-paper) is an unusual piece—the fleur-de-lis border and exotic bird decoration should be noted. The shell is very thickly potted, almost opaque, and very badly fired, so much so that one of the three conical feet upon which it stands is actually burnt, and the entire undersurface covered with black spots. An interesting problem is set by the fact that the decoration takes the form of the well-known Worcester "strawberry" pattern, identical in every respect, but very badly printed. If a copy, there would seem no necessity for such an accurate version; on the other hand, what brought an original copper plate from Worcester to Liverpool? The solution may be that, although the article was certainly not made at Chaffers's factory, the plate may have been brought from Worcester by him. The mug is extremely interesting as a connecting link between several classes of porcelain (see p. 147). Its features are clearly visible in the photograph —the "Heinzelman border", the flower-painting, which includes a charac-teristic convolvulus, and the general poor quality of the paste and glaze. All three pieces are almost opaque, but show a dark yellow in the thinnest parts when viewed by transmitted light.

PLATE 42

a

b

c

PLATE 43

a

d

b   *c*   *e*

PLATE 43

LIVERPOOL

(Zachariah Barnes, *a* and *b*, and Chaffers, *c*, *d*, and *e*)

a TEA-POT. Height, 7 in. Unmarked. About 1770.

b TEA-BOWL AND SAUCER. Diameter (saucer), 4½ in. Unmarked. About 1770.

c COFFEE-CUP. Height, 2¼ in. Unmarked. About 1760–75.

d SAUCER. Diameter, 4 in. Unmarked. About 1760–75.

e TEA-BOWL AND SAUCER. Unmarked. About 1760–75.

N.B. *a*, *b*, are transfer printed

A tea-pot of Barnes's porcelain, conforming in shape to that of a class of coloured pots long supposed to be Liverpool, and in border decoration to a plate which is known to have been made by Barnes (see p. 147). This pot, together with the transfer printed cup and saucer *b*, is similar in paste, glaze, and pigment to the specimens illustrated in Plate 42. The resemblance of the pieces *c*, *d*, and *e* to Worcester cups and saucers is apparent even in the photograph. Chaffers made excellent porcelain, and these specimens are thinly potted, well glazed, and skilfully painted. It is interesting to compare the compositions of the saucer designs, which are identical despite the difference between the subjects.

mentioned, let us now ascertain whether enough is known of any of their products to enable us to make some form of classification.

There is in the Liverpool Museum a mug which was formerly the property of a descendant of Richard Chaffers, and there is reason to suppose that it was in fact made by him. Its body is clean and hard-looking, rather grey, and with a strong green translucency. In every respect the Worcester tradition is followed—the man who received his training at that factory applied what he had learnt to his own products. Using this specimen as a key piece, it is possible to group together a class of Liverpool porcelain which stands apart by reason of its excellence. As already stated, the paste has a green translucency by transmitted light, but in the daylight appears to be grey with a slightly bluish tinge. The glaze is close-fitting, slightly blued, and applied in the Worcester manner with a brush, thus leaving bare patches of glaze inside the foot rim. Cups and saucers are extremely thin, and their foot rims are very often deeply undercut. The blue and white decoration was practically always painted in a slaty blue, which hardly ever ran, so that the drawing is usually extremely clear. The patterns, which were copied from the Chinese, are remarkable for their good composition. Groups of dots used to form part of a pattern are characteristic of an artist whose style is peculiar in this respect. Simple diaper borders were used, the most common being formed of simple trellis-work resembling a repeated letter X, thus: XXXXXXX, of which there are several different forms. Belonging to this factory would appear to be a small class of moulded pieces to which the key-piece is a factory waster, a cup moulded with a feather pattern border with hanging sprays of flowers and foliage over vertical reeding. Such specimens have simple diaper borders, but are otherwise left white (Plate 44). Although there is no evidence to support the assumption, it would appear probable that the porcelain made by Christian after Chaffers's death would be little changed, since the soapstone body had proved to be so entirely successful.

Seth Pennington's blue and white porcelain is characterised by the use of a peculiar blue, often called a "sticky" blue, and probably due to some impurity in the cobalt oxide used in the preparation of the pigment. The term is difficult to explain, but the effect cannot be mistaken—almost as though the colour is, in fact, wet and sticky, and ready to adhere to the fingers if touched. Allied with this is an extremely marked blueing of the glaze, resulting in a duck-egg blue in strong contrast with other porcelains, and in a greenish translucency by artificial light. Moulded patterns were used, usually with reserves for decoration or for the addition of a border. Flat bases were common, but were by no means peculiar to the factory. Indeed, one of a pair of small mugs in my possession had a flat base, whereas the other, which is identical in every other respect, has a low, unground foot rim (Plate 3). Borders peculiar to the factory include one which is formed of circles, with tiny round hubs and spokes radiating to the circumference; a complicated one composed of semicircles enclosing inverted Y's and a series of zigzags below, meeting the point of each Y to form rough fleurs-de-lis; and a variety of the X diaper used by Chaffers, but with alternate panels of foliage. Chinese landscapes and figures were much copied, one of the most common designs being the so-called "Jumping Boy", which was copied from Bow porcelain (Plate 45). Punch-bowls were made, and were decorated with ships in delft style, a form of decoration much favoured by Liverpool potters, as was natural considering the locality.

To Zachariah Barnes has long been ascribed a class of ware heavily potted and decorated with rough prints in dark underglaze blue. That this traditional attribution was correct is now proved beyond any reasonable doubt by the existence of two interesting specimens. The first of these is a thick plate in the Liverpool Museum, to which it was presented by a member of the Barnes family. It is decorated with a Chinese scene in willow pattern style, but its chief interest lies in its diaper border, which is similar to that on the shoulder and cover of the tea-pot shown in Plate 43. The second is a jug in the British Museum which is decorated with printing and painting in blue. On the front, in a reserve of rococo scrolls, is the inscription "Frederick Heinzelman Liverpool 1779", on each side of the spout and amongst the scrolls are liver birds, the emblematic creatures from the city's coat-of-arms, and around the rim is a border of hexagon cell diaper, which is usually known as the "Heinzelman Border" and which can be seen on the mug shown in Plate 42. Although the Heinzelman jug is not

PLATE 44

LIVERPOOL (Chaffers)

a BOWL. Diameter, 6 in. Unmarked. About 1760.

b COFFEE-CUP. Height, 2½ in. Unmarked. About 1760.

Although the paste of each of these specimens of Chaffers's porcelain is like that of Worcester, and possesses its characteristics, the glaze is marred by sanding and spotting, which is clearly visible in the photographs. The bowl has an uncommon but very effective decoration, and the coffee-cup is an example of the moulded decoration whose provenance is proved by a factory waster.

PLATE 44

a

b

PLATE 45

PLATE 45

LIVERPOOL (Pennington's)

COFFEE-CUP AND SAUCER. Diameter (saucer), 4¼ in. Simulated Chinese marks. About 1760.

This attractive cup and saucer, decorated with the "Jumping Boy", is an exact copy of a Bow original; not only of the decoration, but also of the size, shape, moulding, and mark. Its chief characteristic, the excessively blued glaze, is unfortunately invisible in the photograph.

conclusively proved to be of Liverpool origin, the fact that specimens similarly decorated link together in a remarkable manner with the plate already mentioned, serves to provide a nucleus around which a considerable number of pieces may be gathered. In the first place an examination of the tea-pot and mug mentioned above shows clearly that apart from an exact duplication of paste and glaze, there is a remarkable similarity both in the type of printed floral decoration and in the tone of blue in which the printing is executed. There is no doubt whatever of the fact that both pieces came from the same factory, from which it follows that the Heinzelman jug and the Liverpool Museum plate were also made there. Mr. Bernard Rackham, in a paper read to the English Porcelain Circle on February 5th, 1929, showed, in addition to the Heinzelman jug, a cup and saucer of the same body, glaze, and style of decoration. Included in this decoration are prints of the convolvulus and other flowers, which are almost exact duplicates of those on the mug already mentioned, and in addition both cup and saucer have the Heinzelman border. So it links up. Yet another piece of the same class is shown in Plate 42, which depicts a pounce or pepper-pot decorated with birds bearing strong resemblance to the liver birds already mentioned, and with a fleur-de-lis border similar to that often found in conjunction with the Heinzelman border. Thus we have a clearly defined class of blue and white porcelain which has the following characteristics. The potting is heavy and often clumsy, with bluntly triangular foot rims, and unground bases. The paste is yellow in hue by transmitted light, dark straw colour in its thicker parts. The glaze is brilliant, much disfigured by black specks, and seldom blued, giving an appearance of dirty white. Sparrow-beak cream-jugs are common, but have rounded lips, in sharp contrast with the pointed lip favoured at Worcester and Caughley. Tea-pots are invariably larger in size than those made at other factories, with domed covers and pointed knobs. The decoration, as has been already mentioned, is executed in a dark blue, usually printed, and marred by smudges and spots of blue caused by unskilled application. The border found on the Liverpool Museum plate is found in several slightly differing forms, though each includes "fish-roe" diaper in some form or other. Besides the convolvulus, other favourite flowers are the strawberry, anemone, and moss rose. Chinese landscapes usually include a pagoda with strange upturned roofs and large archway beneath, with trees of the type made famous by "willow pattern" styles (Plate 43). Large, thickly potted scallop shells were made, supported on conical feet, with borders of blue wash, and printed floral pattern. Such a one is pictured in Plate 42, decorated with the strawberry or pine-cone design commonly found on Worcester and Caughley wares, although not so well printed. Reference must here be made to a class of ware decorated in overglaze enamels and underglaze blue. A tea-pot of this class was mentioned by Mr. Rackham in the paper already referred to, similar in shape to that shown in Plate 43, but decorated with exotic birds in red, yellow, and blue. The underglaze blue border is exactly similar to that on the museum plate and on the blue and white pot. From this it would appear that such pieces decorated in polychrome should be classed as Barnes's Liverpool, were it not for the fact that the paste and glaze, and the colours used in the decoration, are characteristic of Longton Hall. I have examined many similar specimens, with the result that I am confident that although Barnes undoubtedly added the printed borders, the pieces themselves were potted and painted by Littler (Plate 17). Whether they were printed to his order, or whether Barnes bought the ware at the closure of the Longton Hall factory in 1758 is impossible to decide, although since Barnes flourished during the last quarter of the century the latter possibility is quite feasible.

Apart from the porcelain made by Chaffers and Christian, Pennington, and Barnes, it is difficult to classify the other products of the many Liverpool factories. There are, however, certain traits which enable us to set apart a large number of pieces as of Liverpool origin without any more definite identification. They are as follows:—

1. A moulding of small cabbage leaves around the bases of such articles as tea-pots and mugs, with panels above separated by columns arising from fluted bases and ending in tufts of palm branches. Fragments excavated in Liverpool have done much to discountenance the old supposition that specimens so moulded were made at Longton Hall.

2. A so-called "biting snake" handle. There are two varieties, both taken from silver models. The more complicated one has the upper attachment modelled in the form of a snake's head, the mouth open

as if biting the rim; while the other is formed of one or more scrolls, one end being split in order to bite the rim. Similar handles were used at Worcester.

Finally, it is natural to suppose that with so many factories engaged in the manufacture of delft, earthenware, and porcelain, there will be many hybrids. Such a one is a small class of tin-glazed porcelain, which cannot be definitely attributed to any factory, but which is a natural result of the long association of the city with the manufacture of delft. It is reasonable to suppose that such porcelain would be among the earliest experiments. Indeed, it is certainly a possibility that Zachariah Barnes (who, it will be remembered, gave up the manufacture of porcelain for that of delft) may have attempted the glazing of the new body with the tin glaze with which he was familiar.

Chapter XII

ON COLLECTING

EVERY COLLECTION should have an aim, and every collector should make up his mind exactly what that aim is to be. There is certainly a wide choice; indeed, the collector of blue and white is fortunate in that his field is somewhat restricted, for which reason a finite goal is a real, though perhaps far distant, possibility.

Of course, one might decide to collect out of a natural love of beautiful things, but the fascination of having a definite aim in view will in that case increase the pleasure felt as a result of possessing them. One of the most beautiful collections in existence, the Schreiber Collection in the Victoria and Albert Museum, was made with a view to the gathering together of representative specimens from every English factory. The resultant beauty of the collection is a lasting tribute to the good taste of the lady responsible for its formation.

The possibilities are numerous. For instance, one might collect tea-pots or cream-jugs, and in the case of the former such a collection has actually been made. Against such a choice, however, there is the real danger of monotony; a houseful of tea-pots might easily become quite unbearable! The subject of decoration opens up truly vast possibilities —printed or painted, Chinese figures or flowers, powder-blue, dated or inscribed pieces, and so on—dependent on personal taste and depth of pocket, since dated pieces, for example, are naturally rarer and, therefore, more expensive than ordinary specimens. There are almost unlimited numbers of mouldings, and a collection of moulded articles would be of the greatest interest, inevitably of great beauty, and liable to increase in value. These are but suggestions. I would again stress the importance, nevertheless, of fixing some form of restriction; the quantity of blue and white alone still on the market is so enormous and apparently limitless that, apart from every other consideration, the pleasure which is derived from the search is increased tenfold when

15

one is able, now and again, to secure a single grain from a heap of chaff! The difficulty is not to find the blue and white, but to find first the perfect key-pieces, then the "out-of-the-ordinary", and lastly the curious and rare.

Never, whatever you do, buy broken or cracked specimens, however rare they may be. Dissatisfaction will come sooner or later, and it is improbable that a similar piece will never come your way. Learn to differentiate between fire cracks and accidental damage; the former are wide and will not open if gentle pulling is applied; they are usually filled with glaze, and sometimes covered, or partially so, by handle junctions, applied decoration, etc. Fire cracks are not detrimental, indeed they are often characteristic, and almost welcome for that very reason! It will be found that cups and saucers form by far the greater proportion of the pieces to be found, and care should be taken to avoid amassing too many of them, unless indeed they are being specially collected. They look well in a cabinet entirely devoted to them, but are apt to become monotonous. Unless desirable by reason of shape, decoration, or mark, odd cups should be avoided, since it is a difficult matter to match them with saucers. On the other hand, odd saucers are worth buying, because the appropriate cups will probably turn up. In this connection it is noteworthy that a coffee-cup, a tea-bowl, and a saucer were supplied together, so that all three should be acquired if possible. In the case of tea or coffee-pots it is advisable to resist the temptation to buy any which are lidless, for lids are difficult to find, and a pot without a lid has an unfinished and unpleasing appearance. To a lesser degree the same caution applies to tea-poys (or caddies) and to sucriers (sugar basins), although the latter look well enough as bowls, albeit somewhat out of proportion. Cream-jugs of the sparrow-beak variety were sometimes fitted with covers, but look just as well without them.

There are many sources of supply for the enthusiastic collector. Sometimes the possessors of early blue and white porcelain which has been in the family since its purchase place little value upon it, and judicious admiration, or the offer to replace with something modern and "pretty", may have the desired effect! But such possibilities are usually the dream rather than the reality, and one must perforce look elsewhere. Dealers' shops are of various kinds. At the top of the scale is the specialist, who understands what he is selling, and is able and content to await his price. Many a rarity will come his way, and it will be found necessary to seek his aid more and more as the collection grows. At that stage it will be possible to do this, since the restricted field enables one to buy fewer pieces at higher prices. The general antique dealer, on the other hand, must make his living by the sale of furniture, and porcelain is a sideline. Thus he often knows little about it—everything is "Wall Worcester", and, therefore, infrequently cheap. However, his fixed scale of charges occasionally results in bargains for those who take the trouble to study, since a blue and white tea-pot is to him a tea-pot and nothing more, whether it be decorated with transfer printed flowers or the rare painted "Eloping Bride". Indeed, pieces painted in Chinese style are often offered as Chinese or Japanese at very low prices. An example of this is a Wall coffee-cup of rare "Long Eliza" pattern and even rarer "jade" symbol mark, which was offered to me as Japanese, for sixpence, by a dealer who is an advertised specialist in old Worcester! One of the finest blue and white vases in a famous collection was bought as "some sort of Continental, probably Berlin". Then at the bottom of the scale is the "junk shop". Here everything is filthy, and the contents justify the name. Never ignore such a shop, however, for bargains still lurk amidst the dust and confusion. Open the cupboards, sort the piles of plates, and reach up to the shelves. If anything is found it will be cheap; and remember that a good wash in warm water, with plenty of soap flakes, makes a deal of difference, because dirt collects in the minute scratches in the soft glaze, and disfigures a piece which will appear bright and glistening after its soaking. Do not take a pile of plates or a box full of cups and saucers on its face value—an English piece may be hidden in a pile of Nankin, and very often is, since English replacements were made when Chinese services were damaged.

Despite the pernicious and utterly illegal activities of the "ring", a conspiracy which is familiar to all regular attenders at auction sales, bargains are still obtainable under the hammer. If possible the goods should be carefully "viewed", if not on the previous day, then at least before the commencement of the sale. Here again every separate piece should be examined. Should a good specimen be included in a lot otherwise made up of rubbish, fix your price according to the value of the coveted specimen, and ignore the rest. In any case decide what is to be your limit, and resist the temptation to exceed it. Should you then secure the lot with a dealer as "runner-up" you have probably secured a bargain, since he has to make a profit. Once secured, make sure that your newly acquired property is safe from thieves and from the curious, either by having it locked up, by keeping watch over it, or by taking delivery. Whatever you do, it should not be left on a table or mantelpiece from where it may be easily displaced. It is sometimes impossible to attend a sale in person, in which case, provided the goods have been examined, a bid may be safely left in the hands of a reputable dealer or of the auctioneer. The London sale rooms are prepared to mail catalogues in return for a small annual subscription, and should a desirable specimen be offered for sale it may be viewed on your behalf by one of the many capable and trustworthy specialists, who are prepared to supply a description of the article and an approximate forecast, usually accurate, of the price it is expected to fetch. You may then, if you so desire, advise them, and they will secure, pack, and forward to you, for which service a small commission is charged. Naturally, buying in this way is advisable only if the specimen is one well known to you, and likely to be a desirable addition to your collection.

Untold pleasure may be added to your pursuit by the proper management of your collection. In the first place, apart from the question of proper display—since that aspect of collecting is largely a matter of personal taste and individual circumstance—every specimen should be labelled. For this purpose it is best to have adhesive labels specially printed with your name, together with space for particulars of the factory of origin, approximate date, and catalogue number. Such labels are very cheap and enhance the appearance of a collection, besides giving to it a certain importance! A catalogue is, of course, an absolute necessity. The most suitable form is the loose-leaf variety, in order that insertions may be made, or pages removed in the event of correction, or disposal of specimens. The information which a catalogue contains should comprise particulars of origin, date, mark, full description, reference to similar specimens in famous collections or to illustrations in books, and photographs or sketches. Old copies of collecting magazines should always be purchased, in order that the pictures in the advertisement pages may be cut out and used as illustrations, for which purpose they are ideal. Then a catalogue of marks should be made, in which are sketches of all the marks on your pieces, say half a page for each, together with the catalogue numbers of all the pieces bearing them. An abridged catalogue in which is entered a short description, catalogue number, and mark of each piece, will be found extremely useful if and when the main catalogue overflows to several volumes! Should you be the possessor of a good camera and the necessary skill to make proper use of it, the pieces may be photographed and mounted in an album with accompanying descriptions. It is cheaper to photograph your specimens in groups, taking care to space them widely enough to allow separate enlargement of each. A scrap-book is required in which are pasted those cuttings and notes from journals and magazines which are otherwise easily lost. I have made a practice for some years of taking apart old collectors' journals and rebinding articles on ceramics so as to make handy books of reference.

In conclusion, a good library of books dealing with ceramics is essential. This should include not only recently published works but also the older ones, which, although sometimes out of date and inaccurate as a result, are yet of great value by reason of their illustrations, and because, usually, they are very interesting reading. Catalogues of the leading public collections are obtainable from the museums, and should be acquired. Not only are they authoritative, but the illustrations are invaluable for purposes of comparison and identification. Names of some of the standard books on ceramics are given in the bibliography incorporated in this book.

Chapter XIII

MARKS

IT HAS been pointed out in a previous chapter that the collector should look upon a mark as conclusive if it is supported by the evidence provided by paste, glaze, and decoration. There are, of course, certain marks which are more reliable than others, either by reason of their character or because they are under the glaze, and could not, therefore, have been added at some recent date. Indeed, practically all the marks on blue and white porcelain of the type we are discussing fall into this latter category, and are, therefore, contemporary. Incised marks, or those painted or printed upon the surface of the glaze are always open to suspicion.

There are various sorts of marks, which fall into the following classes: Factory marks, marks copied from other English or foreign porcelains, simulated Chinese marks, inscriptions, and "workmen's marks". Let us consider them in that order.

Factory marks, of which class the Worcester crescent is a good example, were those officially adopted by the proprietors of a factory and intended to serve as a guarantee of the genuineness of the article bearing them. That does not mean to say that unmarked specimens should be viewed with any suspicion. Indeed, it was the custom, especially in later years, to add the mark only to some of the pieces in a service. Chamberlain, for instance, made a practice of marking the lid of the tea-pot in a tea service, or an odd dish or so in a dinner service. Then again, carelessness on the part of the workmen often resulted in the absence of a mark. Many factories used no mark at all, and even those which used a recognised factory mark, as did Worcester, allowed a large proportion of their products to pass into the market unmarked, relying, no doubt, upon the quality of their wares to act as its own guarantee.

It was the practice to make free use of the marks of other factories. Especially was this so when Chinese specimens were imitated, and in this instance I do not think that any fraud was intended. Not only was the design copied, but the project was carried to a logical conclusion by the addition of the appropriate mark. The copyists were no doubt proud of their ability to turn out successful imitations of the much-extolled Chinese porcelain, even though they did not expect their customers to be deceived; since who could have been, taking into consideration the obvious differences in paste and glaze between the original and the copy? Then, again, it was the custom for English buyers to commission the English factories to make replacements to match foreign services, and it was, therefore, necessary to finish such replacements with the proper mark. Not only were the marks upon Chinese porcelain copied, but those on Continental porcelain also, and even those on other English wares. In this latter case, I suspect that fraudulent intent was sometimes present. There can be no other explanation, for example, of the Worcester crescent on a piece of Lowestoft. In other cases, as in that of the same mark upon Caughley porcelain, we have seen that there is an innocent explanation. Naturally enough, many foreign marks have, by reason of their repeated use, been accepted as factory marks. Examples of this are the "square mark" of Worcester, which was a copy of a Chinese seal mark, and the "Chantilly horn" which was copied from the French by both the Worcester and the Caughley factories.

Simulated Chinese marks are commonly found. They are not accurate copies, but by reason of certain flourishes and meaningless strokes, they convey the idea that they are of Eastern origin. Here again we have the pride of the English potter in his success in the attempt to rival the Oriental; or, if we are uncharitable, we may look upon it as his gesture of defiance to what he well knew was the unattainable! Such marks were used at Worcester, Caughley, and Bow.

The various sorts of inscriptions which are found on porcelain sometimes serve as marks although they were not intended as such. Thus, dates are often found either on the bases, incorporated into the scheme of decoration, or even moulded into the body. In this way, even if the factory of origin is not indicated, the date of production very often is. Dates may be written in full, as in the case of a specimen Caughley mug which I have already mentioned, which bears the date "22nd May

1787", or the year only may be denoted, together, maybe, with initials, as for example "SL 1778", which is inscribed within a scroll on the front of another Caughley mug in my possession (Plate 41). A Lowestoft cup and saucer in the Schreiber Collection (Victoria and Albert Museum) has the date 1764, together with the initials IH moulded into its decoration, and so on. Such specimens are valuable in that they offer concrete evidence as to the type of ware produced at that particular date. The actual names of the factory of origin are sometimes found inscribed on porcelain, as witness the famous inkstands of Bow, "Made at New Canton" and the date 1750 or 1751, and the tea-poys of Lowestoft on which is the inscription "A Trifle from Lowestoft".

Lastly, workmen's marks. So-called for want of a better explanation, these marks are small in size and often Chinese in conception, and are found on Worcester, Bow, and Lowestoft wares. They are never found in conjunction with any factory mark. They certainly have no connection with pattern books, since the same mark is often found upon different designs. On the other hand, designs which would appear to have been painted by the same hand sometimes bear different marks. The absence of any sort of record of the patterns and painters of the Worcester factory makes it impossible to arrive at any better explanation of their significance, and we must be content to accept them at their face value.

The reproductions of marks included in this chapter are of those most commonly found, and it is realised that there may be many others, among them those which by reason of their rarity are unlikely to be found on specimens within the reach of the average collector.

WORCESTER

1–5 The crescent is the most common of the Worcester marks, and was probably adopted from the coat-of-arms which was carved over the fireplace in the library of Warmstry House, the first premises used by the Worcester proprietors. The open crescent is found on blue-painted specimens, and is often so misshapen as to lose its true crescent form. The filled-in version is in reality a form of the open crescent, accidentally filled in, and is sometimes found with the horns painted in and the centre left open. Care should be taken to differentiate between this version and the blurred hatched or shaded one. The latter is found only on printed wares. Both the open and hatched crescents are very occasionally found on a single specimen, should the decoration be executed in both painting and printing. On printed wares also is found the hatched crescent with an initial letter, which may be E, L, or R. The crescent with a face is very rare, and is found on printed ware.

6–8 The so-called "square mark" is much sought after, and is usually considered as the hall-mark of the highest workmanship. On blue and white wares it appears to have been reserved for use on specimens decorated in powder-blue, with reserves, and sometimes when so used it is accompanied by an open crescent. There are other forms in addition to those illustrated, and all were copied from a Chinese seal mark.

9–13 The "W" mark. Like the crescent, the W is a factory mark, and was intended to stand either for Worcester or for Wall. There are many written forms, which were used on painted wares, and in addition two printed ones (12 and 13), which were used on printed specimens. In common with the square mark, the W is sometimes found together with the crescent. It is not safe to generalise, but it is usual to find this mark, especially in the case of the written variety, on superior grades of porcelain.

14–15 Nos. 14 and 15 are examples of the imitations of Chinese marks which were used by the factory. Some form of W is often concealed in the characters. No. 14 shares the honour with the square mark of being the usual mark used on powder-blue pieces. Such simulated Chinese marks were often enclosed within a double ring, since it was the common Chinese practice to do so.

16–18 The crossed swords, with or without a numeral, were used by the Meissen (or Dresden) factory for many years as their recognised factory mark. Although copied from a European factory, the mark is found upon specimens bearing every type of decoration. The numeral, which may be either 9, 91, or more rarely 6, is usually found between the blades, although very rarely indeed some form of numeral or letter may be found written between the handles.

19 The Chinese symbol for "jade" was used as a Worcester mark either in the form shown or without the double ring. A smaller version was also used as a workman's mark. It is this mark which, owing to its appearance, was once considered to be the initials of the Bow proprietor, Thomas Frye, and which thus led to many pieces of Worcester being wrongly attributed to the Bow factory.

The remainder of the marks used during the Wall period fall into the category of workmen's marks, and a large selection of them is illustrated overleaf. Many of them are so insignificant as to escape careless scrutiny, and an apparently unmarked specimen should be carefully examined to ensure that the mark is not overlooked.

1 2 3 4 5 6 7 8 9 10

11 12 13 14 15 16 17 18

19

WORCESTER (FLIGHT and FLIGHT AND BARR)

1-3 The Flight period followed upon the end of the Wall period in 1783 and lasted until 1792. Both the crescent and the square mark were used during the first years. In addition, the word FLIGHT was written in underglaze blue, sometimes with a crescent, and after 1789, when a Royal Patent was granted to the factory, with a crown.

4 The Flight and Barr period ended in 1807. During that time, at all events after 1792, when Martin Barr became a partner in the ownership, a new paste was evolved, and the presence of a B scratched in the paste is commonly supposed to denote its use. Occasional use of the crescent was still made.

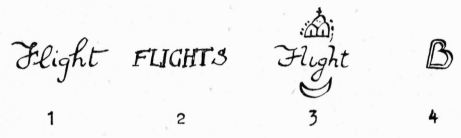

1   2   3   4

CAUGHLEY

1-2 At one time there was considerable doubt as to whether Caughley did in fact make use of the crescent mark, and it was even thought that when found it was actually a poorly formed C. As we have seen, however, blue and white porcelain was made for Worcester by Turner, which fact would account for a proportion of the Caughley crescents. As for the rest, Caughley porcelain was so like that made at Worcester that it is understandable that the proprietors of the former factory might attempt to sell it as such. As at Worcester, the open crescent is found on painted ware, and the printed hatched variety on transfer printed articles.

3-4 The capital C was one of the recognised factory marks. It is found either painted or printed on the appropriate wares.

5-6 The capital S is the other factory mark and is sometimes found with a cross.

7-8 The Caughley imitation Chinese marks are similar to those used at the Worcester factory. The presence of the impressed SALOPIAN on certain powder-blue plates is a final proof of their Caughley origin, although that fact is self-evident from a study of the paste, glaze, and tone of blue. Incidentally, the impressed word was used as a Caughley mark unaccompanied by any other symbol.

9   A copy of the hunting-horn used as a mark by the French factory of Chantilly, Sèvres.

11–16   "Disguised numerals", peculiar to the factory, and printed in many varieties on printed wares, especially when the Turner violet blue is used.

17   A rare mark, impressed, sometimes found together with the capital C.

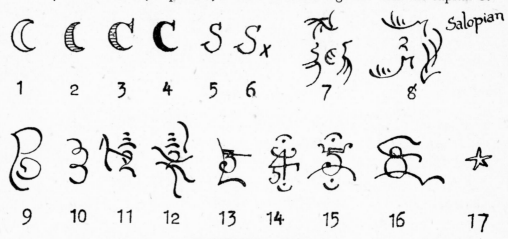

REDCLIFF BACKS

1–3   Incised marks used on the scratch cross family.

4–6   Stamped in raised letters, these marks are very rare, and are found on the few specimens which are the key-pieces to the class of porcelain made at the factory.

Many of the workmen's marks used at Worcester are to be found on Redcliff Backs specimens. Occasionally, also as at Worcester, they are painted beneath the handles of cups or mugs, and should not be overlooked on that account.

LOWESTOFT

Marks found on Lowestoft porcelain pertain to the class known as workmen's marks, and are usually painted on the inside of the foot rim. They are easily overlooked.

1–2 Copies of the Worcester crescent, but much smaller.
3–4 Versions of the Meissen crossed swords.
5–9 Examples of the numbers used in great variety.
10 A copy of the script W of Worcester.
N.B.—No. 2 is found on the small class of transfer printed porcelain attributed to the factory.

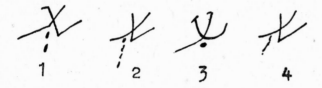

LONGTON HALL

1–4 The only marks used by Littler at Longton Hall, and evidently intended to stand for Littler of Longton. A similar mark is often incorporated in the decoration.

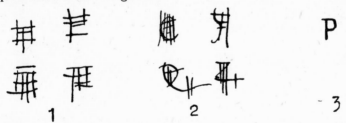

LIVERPOOL

1–2 These marks are found on a hexagonal cup and octagonal saucer in the author's possession, decorated with the famous Bow pattern, the "Jumping Boy". It is probable that both marks and decoration were copied from a Bow original.

DERBY

Very few specimens of Derby blue and white are marked.
1 The mark upon the printed mug which is mentioned in the text as being an attempt by Holdship to print upon Derby porcelain.

2 The most usual mark on blue and white.
3 In blue enamel on a saucer in the Victoria and Albert Museum and on a piece in the collection of the late Frank Hurlbutt.
4 On the handle of a large sauce-boat of the Chelsea Derby period in the author's possession.

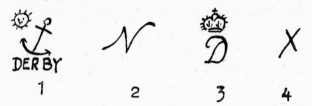

BOW

Blue and white Bow was commonly unmarked, the most usual mark being of the workmen's mark variety. They are not reproduced owing to their similarity to those used at Worcester and Redcliff Backs.

1 Found only on very early specimens.
2 The Chinese symbol for "Jade", once thought to represent the initials of Thomas Frye. Compare with the Worcester variety of the same mark.
3 Considered at one time to be a factory mark.
4–6 Simulated Chinese characters found on powder-blue plates and bowls. Other varieties are common.

Chapter XIV

NOTES ON MATERIALS, MANUFACTURE AND DECORATION

1. METHOD OF TRANSFER PRINTING

The design is in the first place engraved upon a copper plate, a process which results in a reversed picture composed of grooves of varying depth and width, all of them deep enough, however, to hold a quantity of pigment. This pigment is kept warmed and is applied to the whole of the plate by means of a roller or other means, and any surplus is carefully wiped off. A piece of very thin paper is next pressed into contact with the plate in order to transfer the pigment from the engraved lines on to it, thus producing the transfer, which is immediately applied to the biscuit surface of any required article. The paper is pressed well on to the porcelain, after which it is moistened and soaked off, leaving the pigment behind. When the design is dry the article is glazed in readiness for the glost or glazing oven.

It is interesting to note that the present method differs in no respect from that originally perfected at the Worcester factory. The latter was responsible, with the Spode factory, for the introduction of a different process known as "Bat printing", in which dots rather than lines were used to form the design, thus producing a stippled effect. A sheet or bat of glue was used instead of paper for the transfer of the design.

2. SIMPLE POTTING TECHNIQUE

It is desirable that any collector of ceramic wares should have at least a rudimentary knowledge of the potter's craft. Such knowledge can best be obtained by a visit to any modern factory, and in any case the subject is too wide to permit of anything like an exhaustive treatment in these pages. Briefly, however, the chief processes are as follows :—

Throwing on the Wheel. The potter's wheel is one of the oldest and

169

simplest machines known to man. It consists of a horizontal circular table, rotated by hand, foot power, or machinery. A ball of soft clay is placed on its centre, and it is then rotated. The moistened hands are then employed to fashion the desired shape, which may take any form of circular section, depending on the skill of the operator.

Jigger and Jolley Work. Circular dishes, plates, saucers, and cups are made in this manner. The jigger has a revolving head to which moulds may be attached. Clay in the form of a slab or a ball is pressed well into contact with the chosen mould so as completely to cover it. An arm known as the jolley, to which is attached a template of the correct profile, is then swung against the revolving clay, which is thus reduced until the jolley comes against a fixed stop, ensuring the correct thickness of the article. It will be appreciated that the foot rim shape of an article is determined by the design of the moulds and profiles used; a fact which explains why foot rim shapes are important in diagnosis.

Casting. Liquid clay, known as "slip" is poured into a plaster of Paris mould. The water in the slip is absorbed by the plaster, and clay is thus deposited on the interior surface of the mould. When the deposit is thick enough the surplus slip is poured off, and the hollow cast removed when sufficiently dry.

Pressing. Handles, feet, mask lips, and other small parts are made by pressing, and are then fixed to the appropriate articles by means of slip. Clay is pressed into both of the symmetrical halves of the mould, which are then pressed together, provision being made for the escape of any surplus clay.

Firing Biscuit. Articles made by means of these processes are allowed to dry, after which they are fired in a biscuit kiln. They are protected by being placed in rough clay boxes known as "saggars", and are kept apart by the use of stilts, spurs, pads of clay, or other devices.

Glazing. After underglaze decoration has been added to the biscuit surface the article is then glazed. The glaze is in liquid form of the consistency of cream, and it is applied by means of dipping, brushing, or pouring. When dry the ware is placed in saggars and fired in the glost kiln, which works at a lower temperature than the biscuit kiln, and serves to vitrify the powdered glaze.

3. CRAZING

The potter is often confronted with the problem of the marrying together of paste and glaze, since it is necessary that each should expand or contract to the same degree in the glost oven. If they do not, the glaze will not "fit", and the result is a minute network of fine cracks over the surface of the glaze, known as "crazing", which may develop either immediately or at some later date. Although crazing was used by the Chinese to give delightful effects known as "crackle", it is actually a serious disadvantage, as it allows the surface of the ware to become iridescent and then smoky, as well as making it porous.

4. EARLY TECHNICAL DIFFICULTIES

Many of the characteristics which help to determine the origin of old porcelain are really faults which were the result of incomplete mastery of the potter's art. Disfiguring black specks, for instance, were the result of the products of combustion in the kiln being allowed to come into contact with the ware. Wood was sometimes used as fuel, and the use of saggars was not universal. Sanding of the glaze above the foot rim was caused by the sand in which the ware was allowed to stand in order to prevent it from adhering to the kiln. Warping during the firing was extremely prevalent, and was due to two causes: either the body (or paste) had insufficient stiffening matter in its composition, in the shape of bone ash, flint, or fine sand, or else the kiln temperatures were too high, causing the body to become too fluid. Many attempts were made to overcome the instability of the paste, which included the addition of powdered Chinese porcelain, but it was not until the addition of bone ash became universal that a truly reliable body was perfected, although considerable success was attained by the Worcester factory as a result of its use of steatite. Easily fusible clays buckled badly, but on the other hand the harder refractory bodies sometimes remained porous and very often suffered from fire cracks or actual fracture. It is common to see handles that are attached slantwise, a fault due to the inevitable contraction of the body in the kiln. This fault was overcome by the fixing of the handle in its green (unfired) state in an opposite slanting direction, so that it was pulled upright in the kiln, a method still used. Glazes unsuited to any particular body resulted in running or even peeling off, and pigments were affected adversely by certain lead or alkaline bases in the glaze which covered them.

5. CHINESE SHAPES AND FORMS

As in the case of decoration, the early porcelain manufacturer perforce chose the Oriental as his model. It is chiefly as regards ornamental wares and the edges of flat articles such as plates and dishes that this is most noticeable, since much domestic ware (which forms the bulk of blue and white) followed the earthenware shapes already in use.

6. CHINESE DIAPERS

It has been mentioned elsewhere that the diaper borders which are such a feature of blue and white porcelain were in most cases copied from Chinese originals. In turn, these were reproductions of patterns found on bronzes, silks, and brocades.

7. FORGERIES AND IMITATIONS

The comparatively low cost of blue and white porcelain has discouraged the manufacturer of fraudulent imitations, and the factories, notably French, which made a practice of imitating the more valuable polychrome wares have allowed blue and white to escape their attentions. There are certain exceptions, however, of which perhaps the most notable is a class of blue and white earthenware which was produced by Booths of Tunstall in the nineteenth century. Their productions were sometimes marked with their own name, but more often the crescent was used, and the prints with which the ware was decorated were exact copies of those found upon Worcester porcelain. An examination of the paste is all that is necessary in order to detect the deception. Two other classes of reproductions are fairly common. One consists of wavy edged or octagonal plates and leaf-shaped dishes decorated in powder blue, marked with simulated Chinese marks. These are easily mistaken for Bow at a casual glance, but are earthenware. The other class is more dangerous, as it consists of porcelain imitations of Worcester wares, again transfer printed with carefully engraved plates. Such pieces are usually provided with a border formed of large semicircles made up of vertical shading, and are marked with what is best described as a disguised crescent or capital C.

Mention must be made here of the ware known as "clobbered". Genuine blue and white specimens were taken and additional painted decoration added in red and gold, sometimes green, regardless of taste. The second firing necessary for the burning of the additional colours usually resulted in defects in the paste and glaze, among which we find iridescence, crazing, dullness or bubbling of the glaze, and blacking of exposed portions of the body.

8. FRITT PORCELAINS

The fritt porcelains made by the early English factories were of various composition, having in common the fact that all contained a large proportion of glass or "fritt", so called because its ingredients were fused or "fritted" together and then powdered before they were mixed with the chosen clay, whether pipe-clay, calcined bones, calcined shells, or other chalky substance. The fritt itself was sometimes actual glass obtained from a neighbouring glass-house, or else a mixture of substances such as sand, potash, saltpetre, or salt. A small quantity of lead, borax, or other alkaline matter was added to act as a flux, that is, to aid the fusing together of the fritt and the clay.

The addition of soapstone by the western factories, and of bone ash by Bow, Lowestoft, and (to a lesser extent) Chelsea, was found necessary in order to give the body greater strength in the kiln, thus avoiding wastage, the great enemy of all early potters, and to enable it to withstand hot liquids.

Typical recipes of early porcelains are as follows :—

Worcester (Non-steatitic).

  First Fritt.

Sand	4 lb.
Calcined flint	4 lb.
Salt of kelp	1 lb.

  Second Fritt.

First fritt	4 lb.
Bone ashes	4 lb.
Smalt (cobalt ore)	4 oz.

  The Body.

Second fritt	3 lb.
Barnstaple clay	$\frac{1}{4}$ lb.

Worcester (Steatitic).

The Fritt.		*The Body.*	
Sand	10 lb.	Fritt	5 lb.
Calcined flint	6 lb.	Flint glass	5 lb.
Potash	2 lb.	Crown glass	2 lb.
Smalt	$\frac{1}{4}$ lb.	Hard soapy rock	1 lb.
		Soft soapy rock	$4\frac{1}{2}$ lb.

Bow (Frye's patent of 1748).

The Fritt.		*The Body.*	
Burnt chalk, limestone, or other chalky substance	2 parts	Fritt	3 parts
Flint, white pebble, or sand	1 part	Pipe-clay	1 part

9. STEATITE CLAY

The success of the Worcester body, which was virtually unchanged throughout the Wall period, was due to the use of soapstone, steatite, french chalk, soapy rock, or potstone. There is evidence that this substance was used at the Redcliff Backs factory as early as 1750; and in two varieties, hard and soft, at Worcester. A letter from Dr. Pococke, Bishop of Ossory and Meath, provides evidence as to the source of supply and of its use at Bristol. It is as follows:—

> Tavestock in Devonshire,
> 13th October, 1750.

"We went nine miles to the south near as far as Lizard Point, to see the Soapy Rock, which is a little opening in the cliff, . . . they get five pounds a ton for it, for the manufacture of porcelane, now carrying on at Bristol, . . ."

A letter written later in the year, from Bristol, states: "I went to see a manufacture lately established here, by one of the principal [*sic*] of the manufacture at Limehouse which failed. It is at a glasshouse, and is called Lowdin's china house".

10. CHEMICAL ANALYSIS

A full account of the process of chemical analysis of porcelain was published in the *Burlington Magazine* for September 1927, in an article by Mr. Donald MacAlister. The process, developed by Dr. H. J. Plenderleith, does not necessitate any damage to the specimen under examination, and is in reality a method of determining the presence or otherwise of bone ash in the paste, which is denoted by a positive test for phosphoric acid. Briefly, a portion of the body is denuded of glaze, and hydrofluoric acid is added, and allowed to stand for a few minutes. It is then washed off into a solution of ammonium molybdate, to give a yellow reaction should phosphate be present. A further test is described by which the actual percentage of phosphate may be determined. By this means it is possible to separate the bone-ash paste of Bow and Lowestoft from the pastes of other factories.

11. GILDING

It has been pointed out that gilding is usually absent from blue and white porcelain. Its occasional presence, however, warrants some mention of its value as a clue towards correct diagnosis.

At Longton Hall the gilding was applied by means of gold leaf to a sized decoration. It had poor wearing qualities, and is not often seen. Only early factories used honey gilding, that is, a mixture of pure gold and honey was used as a pigment, the latter being burnt away in the kiln. The resultant gilding was soft in appearance, in direct contrast to its modern counterpart, which is applied in the form of a gold and mercury amalgam. In this process the mercury is vaporised, and the resultant gold needs to be burnished. Even a honey gilding, however, may have a brassy appearance if it is applied to a harder porcelain, such as Flight's or Chamberlain's Worcester. Gilding on Chelsea porcelain was thick and soft, and similar to that used at Bow. Wall period gilding was extremely thick, perceptible to the touch, and often with visible brush marks. It was often the practice, especially at the hard paste Bristol factory, to use an undercoating of red enamel over which the gold was added, resulting in a raised effect with a distinct red tint to the gold. Alternatively, a less fine effect, though still raised, was obtained by mixing together the gold and the enamel before application.

12. Wasters on the Bow Factory Site

Mr. Aubrey J. Toppin undertook excavations on the north side of Stratford High Street in June 1921. His labours resulted in the discovery of a large collection of fragments, which included a thick layer of blue and white pieces. Mr. Toppin reports his finds as follows:—

"*Blue and White.* A seam, 5 or 6 inches thick, of blue and white fragments, was found in one hole. . . . The pieces secured were mostly very small. Many, however, were large enough to be instructive for comparative purposes. They included parts of plates, cups and saucers, bowls, tea-pots (several spouts), handles of various shapes, and sauce-boats, some of which had ring-bases that had become detached. The paste and colour shows great variety, the former varying from a very hard body to a soft material easily scratched with a knife—the colour being in many cases a very full blue, and in others of a somewhat pale shade. The designs are all strongly Chinese in character. Floral ornament, often with the peony, predominating; landscapes of the willow pattern type; a few pieces of the powder-blue ground with small landscapes in reserves, such as was made at Worcester and Lowestoft; several small fragments painted with the blue dragon design; and many varieties of diaper patterns for borders of cups and small bowls.

"*Transfer Printing.* No examples of blue transfer printing were found."

13. Robert Hancock

Robert Hancock was born in Burslem in 1731 and died in Bristol in 1817. Apart from his relations with the porcelain factories of Bow, Worcester, and Caughley he was a man of considerable eminence in contemporary art, although very little is known of his exact movements. Tradition has long insisted that Hancock received his training at the Battersea Enamel factory and at Bow, before he went to Worcester, and this is supported by the known facts. The Battersea Enamel works at York House was at one time accepted as having had a comparatively short life of six years, that is, from 1750 to 1756, in which latter year a sale of the factory and stock is known to have been held. Research by Mr. W. B. Honey, however, shows that the actual life of the factory was but three years, from 1753 to 1756, and that enamels made after that period were probably made in Birmingham, perhaps with the help of ex-Battersea workmen.

During some part of this short life Hancock must be presumed to have studied line engraving under the skilled engraver, Ravenet. In support of this presumption there is a Battersea enamel watch back in the museum attached to the Royal Porcelain Works at Worcester, decorated with a transfer print of "The Tea Party", a design which was afterwards made famous by Hancock when he worked at Worcester. The print on the watch back is signed "R.H., f", which obviously means Robert Hancock, fecit. Mr. Honey has expressed his distrust of this evidence, pointing out, quite rightly, that the decoration could have easily been added at Worcester. Instead, he puts forward as evidence of Hancock's work at Battersea three well-known prints which are to be found on enamels originating there, and which by reason of their style and technique could have been engraved by no one else. The three patterns in question are "Les Amours Pastorales", after Boucher, "Le Calendrier des Vieillards", and a print of a man and a woman walking in a landscape.

At the closing of the Battersea factory in 1756 it must be supposed that Hancock went to the Bow porcelain factory; although, since there is evidence that he was working at Worcester in 1757, his stay must have been a very short one. As evidence of his work there, a plate decorated with a print of "L'Amour" is often quoted, because, as in the case of the "Tea Party", the subject is well known as one of his Worcester successes. The reliability of this evidence was disputed by Mr. Frank Tilley on the grounds of style and execution. Instead, Mr. Tilley compared a Bow plate printed in red transfer with the subject of "Æneas and Anchises", with a Worcester mug bearing decoration which was obviously produced from the identical engraved plate. There is no doubt whatever of the authenticity of the two specimens, or of the fact that the engraving was done by Hancock.

As has already been mentioned, Hancock went to Worcester soon after 1756, and the famous "King of Prussia" mugs, dated 1757, are fairly well proved to have been printed with his engravings. He was made a partner of the business in 1772, but left two years later, having saved about £6,000 which he was to lose shortly afterwards in a Staffordshire bank failure. His printed designs have never been surpassed and seldom equalled, combining as they do a high degree of good taste and wellnigh perfect technique. The large majority of his patterns are adaptations of the Masters, among which are found Le Brun, Collet, Rembrandt, etc., while others are versions of engravings printed in contemporary books of design.

Mention has already been made in another chapter of the fact that although Hancock's engravings were primarily intended for use with overglaze enamels, some of them were afterwards used in underglaze blue, with a natural loss of that clear, sharp definition which is outstanding in all his work.

14. BORDERS (Figs. 1–3)

The majority of the borders pictured are of Chinese origin, and they were naturally copied by various factories, who in turn copied from each other. The selection shown here makes no claim to be comprehensive—there are many others differing only in detail from those chosen for reproduction. It should be realised, moreover, that some of them may be found on specimens originating in factories other than those mentioned.

BOW.   d, dd, ll.
CHELSEA.   d.
CHELSEA DERBY.   oo.
CAUGHLEY.   e, k, m, ee, ff, hh, jj.
DERBY.   kk.
LIVERPOOL.   d, f, r, y, z, aa, bb, cc, dd, gg, ii.
LOWESTOFT.   l, s, t, u, v, w, x, nn.
WORCESTER.   a, b, c, d, e, f, g, h, i, j, k, m, n, o, p, q, dd, mm.

Although many of the borders are found in both printed and painted form, the following are usually printed :—

e, n, bb, cc, ee, ff, hh, ii, and jj.

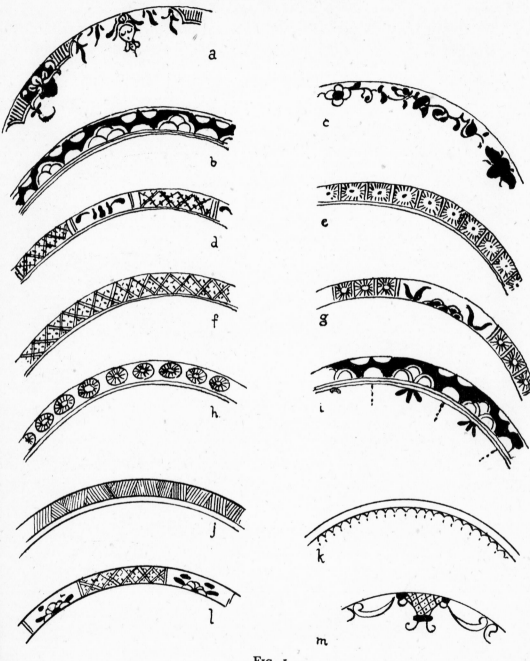

FIG. 1

FIG. 2

180

FIG. 3

	CHELSEA	BOW	LONGTON HALL	DERBY
1740	Thomas Briand, 1740–3. Fritt porcelain.			
1745		Thos. Frye and Heylyn, 1744–45.		Traditional founding
		Fritt porcelain.		1745 (?).
	Nicholas Sprimont.	Frye's bone-ash body and Heylyn gone, 1749.		
1750				Inscribed and dated pieces, 1750. Fritt porcelain.
		"New Canton" with Weatherby and Crowther. Warehouse at Cornhill, 1753.	First advertisement, 1752 Fritt porcelain.	
	Auction sale, 1754.			
1755	Sprimont ill, 1756. Some workmen to Bow and Worcester. Bone ash paste, 1758. Sprimont recovered.	Bowcocke's first Mem. Book, 1756. First auction, 1757. Frye leaves, 1759.	First auction, 1757. Last auction, 1758.	Heath, Planche, and Duesbury, 1756. London auctions, 1756–7. Longton bought (?), 1758 Holdship joins staff, 1759.
1760	Sprimont ill, 1763–4.	Death of Weatherby, 1762. Crowther bankrupt, 1763. Sale of stock, 1764. Death of Bowcocke, 1765.	Probably bought by Duesbury, 1758.	
1765				
1770	Death of Sprimont.	Crowther opens St.		Chelsea bought.
	Factory bought by Duesbury of Derby, 1770.	Paul's Churchyard warehouse. Works almost closed.		Chelsea-Derby period, 1770–84. Bone ash added to paste. ↑ ↑ ↑
1775				
		Stock taken to Derby by Duesbury, 1776.		
1780				
1785				
1790				
1795				
1800				

THE RESPECTIVE FACTORIES, 1740–1800.

LOWESTOFT	REDCLIFF BACKS	WORCESTER	CAUGHLEY	LIVERPOOL	
					1740
					1745
	Jas. Davis and Edward Heylyn, 1745. Steatite porcelain. Dated pieces, 1750.				1750
	Lyes and Podmore to Worcester, 1751.	"Worcester Tonquin Manufactory," 1751. Steatite porcelain.	Pottery founded 1750. Gallimore, 1754. Made earthenware.		
	Transferred to Worcester, 1752.				
Walker, Browne, Aldred, and Richman, 1757. Bone ash paste.		London warehouse, 1756. Underglaze blue printing, 1757–60.		Richard Chaffers' advertisement, 1756. Sadler and Green (printing discoveries).	1755
					1760
					1765
Robt Browne & Co., 1770		Two London sales, 1769.			1770
		Hancock goes, 1774.	Thos. Turner, 1772. Steatite porcelain.		1775
		Dr. Wall dies, 1776.		"Heinzelman" jug, 1779.	1780
		Joseph and John Flight. Chamberlain leaves, 1783.	London warehouse, 1783.		
					1785
		George III visit to works, 1788.			1790
		John Flight dies, 1791. Martin Barr joins firm, 1792.			1795
		Bone ash paste.			
			Sold to Coalport, 1799.		1800
Factory closed, 1802.					

BIBLIOGRAPHY

THE NAMES of many well-known books on ceramics are missing from this short bibliography for no other reason than that they are lacking in information relating to blue and white decoration.

The books mentioned here should be regarded as forming a nucleus, to which others may be added as and when they may be obtained, for books on all branches of collecting are both scarce and expensive.

In addition, valuable and interesting information can be found in back numbers of the *Connoisseur, Burlington, Antique Collector,* and *Apollo,* and in the *Transactions* of the English Ceramic Circle and the English Porcelain Circle.

Bemrose, W. "Bow, Chelsea, and Derby Porcelain." London, 1898.

Binns, R. W. "Catalogue of a Collection of Worcester Porcelain in the Museum at the Royal Porcelain Works." Worcester, 1882.

Blunt, R. "Cheyne Book of Chelsea China." London, 1924,

Bryant, G. E. "Chelsea Porcelain Toys." London, 1925.

Church, Sir A. H. "English Porcelain." London, 1904.

Hobson, R. L. "Catalogue of the Collection of English Porcelain in the British Museum." London, 1905.

Hobson, R. L. "Worcester Porcelain." London, 1910.

Honey, W. B. "Old English Porcelain." London, 1928.

Honey, W. B. "The Art of the Potter." London, 1944.

Hurlbutt, F. "Bow Porcelain." London, 1927.

Hurlbutt, F. "Bristol Porcelain." London, 1928.

Jewitt, L. "Ceramic Art of Great Britain." London, 1878.

King, W. "Chelsea Porcelain." London, 1922.

Nightingale, J. E. "Contributions towards the History of Early English Porcelain." Salisbury, 1881.

Pountney, W. J. "Old Bristol Potteries." Bristol, 1920.

Rackham, Bernard. "Catalogue of the Schreiber Collection of English Porcelain." (Vol. 1.) London, 1928.

Rackham, Bernard. "Catalogue of the Herbert Allen Collection of English Porcelain." London, 1923.

Spelman, W. W. "Lowestoft China." Norwich, 1905.

Turner, W. "Transfer Printing on Enamels, Porcelain, and Pottery." London, 1907.

INDEX

"Æneas and Anchises" pattern, 177
Analysis, chemical, of porcelain, 6, 174
Anchor mark 41
Applied flowers, 10, 15, 20, 54, 100
Artificial porcelain, 1

"B," incised mark, 117, 165
Barnes, Zachariah, 64, 141, 145, 147
Barnes' border, 145 (Pl. 43)
Barr, Martin, 79
Baskets, 10, 15, 47, 50, 85, 100 (Pls. 2, 13)
Bat printing, 169
Battersea enamels, 101, 176
Bird subjects—
    Caughley, 120, 126, 139
    Chelsea, 41
    Liverpool, 142
    Longton Hall, 65
    Worcester, 84, 118
Bone-ash, 2, 40, 42, 141, 173
Bow—
    borders, 33
    decoration, 29 (Pls. 6, 7, 8, 9)
    excavations on factory site, 29, 176
    experimental period, 23
    flower-painting, 27, 29
    glaze, 23, 28
    handles, 4, 15, 28
    history, 23
    inkpots, inscribed, 24
    marks, 29
    moulded wares, 27 (Pl. 7)
    mugs, 28 (Pls. 7, 9)
    octagonal plates, 28 (Pl. 2)
    opalescence, 28
    paste, 23, 28
    powder-blue, 34 (Pl. 2)
    transfer printing, 29
    wasters, 29, 176
Bowcocke, John, 29
Bowls, punch, 147
Bradley, Samuel, 15, 85
Briand, Thomas, 39

Bristol—
    decoration, 15
    flower-painting, 72
    glaze, 69
    hexagonal boats, 71, 73 (Pl. 18)
    history, 68
    marks, 69, 70
    moulded wares, 71 (Pl. 18)
    paste, 69
    "scratch cross" family, 70
British Museum, 147
"Broseley Dragon" pattern, 95, 135
Browne, Robert, 42
Brownhills, 60
Bryant, Thomas, 39
Burlington Magazine, 174
Burnished gold, 175
Butterfly decoration, 14, 118, 135

"C" mark, 165
Cabbage leaf jugs, 20, 47, 85, 91, 99, 126
    (Pls. 27, 31, 38)
Caddy-spoons, 85, 91
Canton, New, 8, 23
Casting, 170
Castle Green, 69
Catalogues, how to keep, 158
Caughley—
    borders, 19, 135
    decoration, 135 (Pl. 10
    flower-painting, 135
    glaze, 134
    history, 119
    impressed mark, 10
    marks, 120, 133
    moulded wares, 133 (Pls. 4)
    mugs, 133
    paste, 4, 134
    powder-blue, 129, 139 (Pls. 2, 39)
    transfer printing, 124, 134
Chaffers, Marks and Monograms, 42
Chaffers, Richard, 141, 145
Chamberlain, connection with Caughley, 124

Chamberlain's Worcester, 79
Chantilly mark, 161, 166
"Chantilly sprig" pattern, 106, 118, 130, 136 (Pls. 30, 41)
"Charlotte, Queen," pattern, 100, 117 (Pl. 35)
Charlotte, Queen, visit to Worcester, 100
Chelsea—
    decoration, 40
    glaze, 40
    "goat and bee" jugs, 35
    history, 35
    marks, 35, 41
    paste, 4, 39, 41
Chelsea-Derby, 39, 55, 56
Chemical analysis, 6, 174
China-clay, 1
China-stone, 1
Chinese "Chippendale," 14
    influence on decoration, 8, 95, 100
    landscapes, 9, 29, 41, 47, 55, 71, 84, 100, 114, 118, 147, 153 (Pls. 5, 27)
    figures, 8, 55, 95, 100, 147 (Pls. 13, 25, 28)
    marks, simulated, 29, 34, 120, 139, 160, 163, 168
"Chippendale, Chinese," 14
Christian, Philip, 141, 146
Chronological Table, 182
Church, Professor, 39, 184
Circle, impressed, 134
Clobbered ware, 173
Coalport, 124
Cobalt blue, 2
Collect, how to, 155
Commemorative pieces, 47
Conical feet, 66, 142
Cornucopia, 80 (Pls. 19, 20)
Crazing, of glaze, 53, 84, 171
Crescent mark, 160, 165, 167
Cross mark, 56, 70
Crossed swords mark, 99, 163
Crowther, John, 23

"D" mark, 168
Dated pieces, 48, 161 (Pl. 41)
Davis, William, 68, 79
Delft—
    Bristol, 15
    Liverpool, 154
Derby—
    baskets, 50, 54 (Pl. 13)

Derby—continued.
    borders, 55
    flower-painting, 55
    glaze, 54
    handles, 54
    history, 49
    Longton Hall, connection with, 49, 54
    marks, 59
    paste, 54
    patch marks, 49
    transfer printing, 59
Diaper borders, 19, 33, 47, 48, 55, 90, 105, 106, 118, 126, 135, 142, 145, 146, 147, 152, 172, 178, 179, 180, 181
Difficulties, technical, 171
Discoloration of glaze, 28
"Dragon" pattern, 8, 29, 95
Dresden porcelain, 14
"Duck-egg" blue, 13, 45, 147
Duesbury, William, 23, 39, 49, 60
Dutch influence, 14, 46
Dyson-Perrins Collection, 29, 84, 118, 124, 133

Earthenware imitations, 172
Edkins, Michael, 15
Egg-drainers, 85, 86, 91 (Pl. 22)
Egg-shell porcelain, 89, 91
Elers brothers, 15
Elliott, Wallace, 69
"Eloping Bride" pattern, 8, 100, 157
Enamel, white, 42, 67
English landscape decoration, 14, 120
Examining porcelain, 5
Excavations—
    at Bow, 29, 176
    at Liverpool, 153
    at Lowestoft, 46
Exotic birds, 142, 153 (Pl. 17)

Factory marks, 160
Figures, Chinese, in decoration, 8, 55, 95, 100 (Pls. 13, 25, 28)
"Fir-cone" pattern, 101, 114, 142, 153 (Pls. 33, 34, 42)
Fire cracks, 62, 66, 156
"Fisherman" pattern, 16, 120, 129 (Pls. 4, 5)
"Fish-roe" diaper, 50, 152
"Fleur-de-lys" border, 19, 142, 152
"Flight" mark, 165

Flight period, 79, 117
Flight, Thomas, Joseph, and John, 79
Flowers, moulded, applied, 10, 15, 20, 54, 100
Flower-knobs, 20, 47, 100, 130
Flower-painting, 27, 29, 48, 55, 67, 72, 100, 135, 142
Fluted patterns, 85
Foot rims, 4, 28, 40, 134, 146, 170
Forged marks, 4, 160
Forgeries of blue and white porcelain, 172
Fretted square mark, 161, 163
Frit (or Fritt), 1, 173
Fruit-painting, 14, 114, 126
Frye, Thomas, 23, 68, 163, 168

"G" mark, 27, 34
Gainsborough, 14, 135
Gallimore, 119
George III, visit to Worcester, 100
Gilbody, Samuel, 141
Gilding, 67, 100, 135, 175
Glass House, Lowdin's, 68
Glazes, 2
Glazing, method of, 170
Glost oven, 169
Glue Bat printing, 169
Goat and bee jugs, 35
Gold decoration, 175
Gouyn, Charles, 35
Granulated blue, 55
Green, Valentine, 101
Grooved handles, 90
Ground foot rims, 84
Ground Oriental porcelain, 24
Ground, powder-blue, 9, 10, 34, 48, 90, 100, 129, 139 (Pls. 2, 11, 39)

Hancock, Robert, 8, 100, 119, 135, 176
Handles, distinctive, 4, 15, 20, 66, 71, 100, 153
Hard paste, 1
Hatched crescent mark, 162
Hawthorn blossom, 9, 100 (Pl. 28)
Heart-shaped handle terminal, 33 (Pl. 9)
Heath, John, 39, 49, 60
"Heinzelmann" border, 142, 147, 152 (Pl. 42)
Hexagonal boats, 71 (Pl. 18)
Hexagonal cups and saucers, 85 (Pl. 10)
Hexagonal diaper, 147

Heylyn, Edward, 23, 68
Hodgson, Mrs. Willoughby, 61
Holdship, Richard, 7, 59, 167
Honey, W. B., 54, 176, 184
Honey gilding, 175
Horn mark, 166
"Hundred Antiques" pattern, 8, 83, 100 (Pl. 21)
Hunting scenes, 14
Hurlbutt, Frank, 24, 84, 168, 184

Identification of porcelain, suggested procedure, 5
"Image" pattern, 8, 22, 29 (Pl. 6)
Imitations of blue and white, 172
Impressed marks, 10, 139, 165
Indigo blue, 29, 100
Inkpots, inscribed, 24, 46
Inscriptions on porcelain, 14, 46, 162 (Pl. 41)
Iridescent glaze, 28

Jackfield pottery, 119
Jade, Oriental character mark, 34, 95, 157, 163, 168
Japanese porcelain, copies of, 9
Jewitt, Llewellyn, 124, 141, 184
Jigger and Jolley work, 170
Jugs—
    cabbage leaf, 20, 47, 85, 91, 99, 126 (Pls. 27, 31, 38)
    goat and bee, 35
    mask, 20, 47, 85, 91, 109, 126 (Pls. 31, 38)
    sparrow-beak, 90, 152 (Pl. 36)
"Jumping Boy" pattern, 8, 29, 147, 151 (Pl. 45)

Kakiemon style, 9
Kaolin, 1
K'hang H'si, 3, 8
"King of Prussia" mugs, 177
Knife-handles, 46, 85

"L," double, mark, 167
"L'Amour" pattern, 177
Landscape painting (see Chinese landscapes)
"Lange Lizsen," 8, 55, 95, 100 (Pls. 13, 25, 28)
Lead glaze, 2, 84

Leaf-shape wares, 20, 66 (Pls. 4)
"Lily" pattern, 100, 117 (Pl. 35)
Limehouse porcelain, 68, 174
Littler, William, 60
Littler blue, 16, 55, 62, 66
Liverpool—
    borders, 145, 146, 147
    decoration, 142, 146, 151, 152, 153
    excavations on factory site, 153
    factories, 141
    flower-painting, 142
    glaze, 142, 146, 148, 152
    handles, 4, 153
    history, 140
    marks, 167
    moulded wares, 146, 148
    mugs, 143, 146 (Pls. 3, 42)
    paste, 142, 146, 152
    transfer printing on Longton Hall wares,
      65, 67, 153 (Pl. 17)
    wasters, 148, 153
"Liver" birds, 152 (Pl. 42)
"Long Eliza" patterns, 8, 55, 95, 100 (Pls. 13,
    25, 28)
Longton Hall—
    baskets, 61
    borders, 67
    connection with Derby, 60
    connection with Liverpool, 65, 67
    decoration, 66
    flower-painting, 67
    glaze, 66
    handles, 66
    history, 60
    marks, 167
    moulded wares, 66 (Pls. 4, 16)
    mugs, 62, 67 (Pl. 16)
    paste, 61
    salt-glazed wares, 60, 66
    "streaky blue," 16, 62, 66 (Pls. 4, 16)
    transfer printing, 67 (Pl. 17)
Loop handles, 90
"Love Chase" pattern, 8
Lowdin's Glass House, 68
Lowestoft—
    birth tablets, 48
    borders, 47, 48
    "Chinese," 42
    decoration, 45, 47 (Pls. 11, 12)
    excavations at, 46
    flower-painting, 48
    glaze, 42, 46

Lowestoft—continued.
    "hard paste," 42
    history, 42
    inscribed porcelain, 45, 46, 47
    marks, 166
    miniature pieces, 46
    moulded wares, 45 (Pls. 4, 12)
    paste, 42
    powder-blue, 48 (Pl. 11)
    transfer printing, 48 (Pl. 12)
    wasters, 46
Lucock, John, 141
Lyes, 69, 79

Mackenna, Dr. F. Severne, 35
Manganese purple, 2
Marks—
    factory, 160
    impressed, 10
    incised, 70
    inside foot rim, 166
    simulated Chinese, 4, 29, 83, 160
    unreliable nature of, 160
    workmen's, 34, 70, 162, 163, 166, 168
Mask jugs, 20, 47, 85, 91, 109, 126 (Pls. 31,
    38)
Mason, Miles, 141
Meissen, 14, 118, 167
Mercury-gold gilding, 175
"Milkmaid" pattern, 110, 118, 135 (Pl. 32)
Miniature wares, 46
"Moons," 39, 54, 66
Moulded wares, 4, 15, 20, 46, 66, 84, 85, 92,
    118, 133, 146, 148
Moulds, 4, 20, 170
Mugs, distinctive shapes, 32, 62, 66–67, 91
    (Pls. 3, 9, 16, 23)
Musselburgh, 62

"N" mark, 168
Nankin porcelain, 28, 157
"New Canton," 8, 23, 162
Nightingale, J. E., 60, 184
Numerals, disguised, 120, 166

Octagonal plates, 28, 90 (Pl. 2)
Opalescent glaze, 28
Opaque porcelain, 28, 66, 69, 142
Open crescent mark, 162

INDEX

Openwork patterns, 10, 47
Oriental figures, 8 (Pls. 13, 25, 28)
Overglaze printing, 101

"P" mark, 167
Pale blue, 29, 50, 53, 55
"Panini Ruins" pattern, 135
"Parrot and Vine" pattern, 13, 118, 126,
    133, 135 (Pl. 38)
"Partridge" pattern, 9, 16 (Pl. 4)
Pastes—
    description of, 23, 28
    hard and soft, nature of, 1
    recipes of, 173
"Patch" family, 49
Pennington, Seth, 141, 146, 151
Peony, in decoration, 29, 30, 71 (Pls. 7, 8, 9)
Perrins, Dyson, Collection, 29, 84, 118, 124,
    133
Petuntse, 1
"Pheasant" pattern, 120
Phosphate, test for, 174
Pickle trays, 16, 20, 66, 71, 85 (Pls. 4, 42)
Pierced patterns, 10, 15, 47, 50, 85, 100
"Pine-cone" pattern, 101, 114, 142, 153
    (Pls. 33, 34, 42)
Pipe-clay, 173
Planché, Andrew, 49, 60
Pococke, Dr. Richard, 68, 174
Podmore, 69, 79
Porcelain, nature of, 1
Potter's wheel, use of, 169
Powder-blue, 9, 10, 34, 48, 90, 100, 129, 139
    (Pls. 2, 11, 39)
Pressing, method of, 170
Printing—
    bat, 169
    overglaze, 7, 101
    underglaze, 7, 101
Prussian blue, 67
Punch-bowls, 147

"Quail" pattern, 9, 16
"Queen Charlotte"—
    pattern, 100, 117 (Pl. 35)
Queen Charlotte—
    visit to Worcester, 100

Rackham Bernard,, 152, 184

Recipes for making porcelain, 173
Redcliff Backs (see Bristol).
Refiring, effects of, 173
Reid & Co., 141
Rims, foot, shapes of, 4, 28, 40, 134, 146, 170
Rope-shaped handles, 50 (Pl. 13)
Rose, John, 124
Ross, James, 101
"Royal Lily" pattern, 100, 117 (Pl. 35)
"Rural Lovers" pattern, 14

"S" mark, 133, 165
Sadler and Green, 7, 141
Saggars, 170
Sales, buying at, 157
Salopian porcelain (see Caughley).
Salt-glaze, 60, 66, 80
Sandys, Lord, 76
Sauce-boats, two-handled, 85, 89, 90 (Pl. 23)
Saucers, scarcity of, 156
Scallop shell moulds, 16, 20, 71, 153
Scratch "B" mark, 165
Scratch cross family, 70, 166
Seal mark, 163
Sections of foot rims, significance of, 4
Shapes, Chinese, 20, 172 (Pl. 1)
Shell, scallop, 142 (Pl. 4)
Ships used for decoration, 48, 147
"Shou," 53
Silver shapes copied, 4, 15
Slip, use of, 170
Smalt, 173
Soapstone paste, 2, 69, 79, 134, 173, 174
Soft paste defined, 1
"Sparrow-beak" jugs, 90, 120, 152, 156
    (Pl. 36)
Spode, Josiah, 2
Spode porcelain, 2, 169
Spoons, porcelain, types of, 85, 91
Sporting prints, 14
Sprimont, Nicholas, 15, 35
Spur marks, 28
Square mark, 161, 163
Staffordshire porcelain, 60
Star mark, 166
Steatite paste, 2, 69, 79, 134, 173, 174
St. Cloud porcelain, 39
"St. George and the Dragon" pattern, 8,
    100, 118
"Sticky blue," 13, 146

Stilts, use of, 49
Stipple prints, 169
"Strawberry" pattern, 101, 114, 142, 153 (Pls. 33, 34, 42)
Sun-face mark, 168
Sweetmeat-trays, 16, 20, 71, 85 (Pl. 4)
Swords, crossed, mark, 99

"Tea party" pattern, 177
Tea-pots, shapes of, 19, 117 (Pl. 5)
Tea-pot lids, 42
Technical difficulties, 171
Tests for hard paste, 5
"TF" mark, 29
Throwing of porcelain, 169
Tilley, Frank, 54, 177
Tin-glazed porcelain, 2
"Tonquin Manufacture," 8, 79
Toppin, Aubrey J., 176
Transactions, English Porcelain Circle, 184
Transfer printing, 100, 169, 176
Translucency, used as a test, 5
Transmitted light, use of, 5
Trays, sweetmeat or pickle, 16, 20 (Pl. 4)
Trial piece, Caughley, 123, 133 (Pl. 37)
"Trifle from Lowestoft," 46, 162
True porcelain, nature of, 1
Turner, Thomas, 16, 79, 101
Turner, William, 7, 184
Turner-Chamberlain co-operation, 124
Two-handled sauce-boats, 85, 89, 90 (Pl. 23)
"Two Milkmaids" pattern, 110, 118, 135 (Pl. 32)

Undercut foot rims, 146
Underglaze colours, 2
Unequal mixing of fritt, 4

Vases, large blue and white, 84
Violet-blue, 47, 55, 118, 120, 124, 126, 134, 139

"W" mark, 163, 167
Wall, Dr. John, 76
Wall period, 79
Warmstry House, 79
Warped pieces, 50, 54
"Warrior and Dragon" pattern, 8
Wasters—
    from Bow site, 29, 176
    from Liverpool site, 148, 153
    from Lowestoft site, 46
Weatherby, 23
Wedgwood factory, 134, 141
Wheel, potter's, use of, 169
White enamel decoration, 42, 67
Willow pattern, 9, 48, 135, 147, 153
Worcester—
    baskets, 85, 100 (Pl. 2)
    borders, 90, 105, 106, 118
    connection with Caughley, 90, 124
    connection with Liverpool, 101, 141
    connection with Redcliff Backs, 79
    decoration, 100
    flower-painting, 100
    glaze, 84
    handles, 85, 90, 91, 154
    history, 76
    marks, 162
    moulded wares, 85, 91, 92, 100, 118
    mugs, 85, 89, 91, 102 (Pls. 3, 23)
    octagonal plates, 90 (Pl. 2)
    paste, 3, 79
    powder-blue, 90, 100 (Pl. 2)
    spoons, 85
    transfer printing, 101, 113
Workmen's marks, 34, 70, 162, 163, 166, 168
Worn copper plates, use of, 133
"Wreathing" in paste, 171

York House, 176

LIBRARY